Easy English Grammar
STEP-BY-STEP

Related titles:
Easy Writing Skills Step-by-Step
ESL Demystified

Easy English Grammar
STEP-BY-STEP

Master High-Frequency Skills
for Grammar Proficiency—*FAST!*

Second Edition

Phyllis Dutwin

Jane Burstein

New York Chicago San Francisco Athens London Madrid
Mexico City Milan New Delhi Singapore Sydney Toronto

1 2 3 4 5 6 7 8 9 10   LCR   27 26 25 24 23 22

ISBN   978-1-264-87808-6
MHID   1-264-87808-7

e-ISBN   978-1-264-87848-2
e-MHID   1-264-87848-6

List of homographs in Chapter 10 from www.FictionFactor.com; reprinted with permission. Appendix A, "100 Most Often ~~Mispelled~~ Misspelled Words in English," reprinted here by permission. Copyright 2004, Lexiteria LLC and alphaDictionary.com.

McGraw Hill products are available at special quantity discounts to use as premiums and sales promotions or for use in corporate training programs. To contact a representative, please visit the Contact Us pages at www .mhprofessional.com.

McGraw Hill is committed to making our products accessible to all learners. To learn more about the available support and accommodations we offer, please contact us at accessibility@mheducation.com. We also participate in the Access Text Network (www.accesstext.org), and ATN members may submit requests through ATN.

Contents

Preface

Welcome to *Easy English Grammar Step-by-Step*. By purchasing this book, you have already taken the first important step: You have made the decision to improve your spoken and written English.

Everyone wants to present themselves in the best possible way, and avoiding common errors in spoken and written English is a step towards this goal. And, while *Easy English Grammar Step-by-Step* teaches some basic grammatical terms and definitions, it does much more than that. This book teaches you to take what you've already learned and apply that knowledge to help you recognize and avoid common errors in spoken and written English.

How to Use This Book

Easy English Grammar Step-by-Step presents skills gradually. The chapters build upon each other. Consequently, the best way to use this book is to begin with Chapter 1 and continue with the chapters one after the other. Only Chapter 11, "Spelling," and Appendix A, "100 Most Often ~~Mispelled~~ Misspelled Words in English," should be taken out of order. While spelling rules can be presented in one chapter, they certainly can't be learned in one sitting. In fact, it is a good idea to study spelling in small doses. You can begin studying these chapters early and continue studying them on a regular basis.

There are short exercises throughout the book and a longer exercise at the end of each chapter. Be sure try each one of them and then consult the Answer Key to follow your progress. If you find you are still having difficulty with a grammatical concept or skill, go back and reread the chapter until you feel more confident in your knowledge.

Easy English Grammar Step-by-Step emphasizes the difference between two levels of English—*informal* and *standard*. Although both are correct in the right environment, you don't want to confuse the different levels of spoken and written English. We all speak or write to friends and family in an informal way (usually in emails or texts), but being informal is not always appropriate, especially if you're writing a report for school or a résumé for a summer job. In those situations, your teacher or prospective employer will expect to read Standard English.

INFORMAL: Running late. Catch up later?
STANDARD: I will be unable to be there by 1:00. May I call you later?

INFORMAL: Great dinner! Again next week?
STANDARD: I enjoyed our dinner. Do you want to meet again next week?

When in doubt, choose the standard level of English.

Easy English Grammar
STEP-BY-STEP

1

Always Right:
The Complete Sentence

The English language gives speakers and writers so many ways to express their thoughts. In a formal situation, however, one rule always applies. We help our readers and listeners understand our thoughts by using complete sentences. You'll learn the basics of complete sentences in this chapter.

Choose Standard English

As the Preface explained, we often use informal English when we're communicating with friends and family. With informal English, we feel free to use incomplete sentences. That's not the case with Standard English. In school or at work, we communicate with teachers, customers, and employers using Standard English. We need to be flexible language users, making choices depending on the situation.

In this chapter, you'll learn one of the main requirements of Standard English: the complete sentence. Informal English allows us to use incomplete sentences. Standard English does not.

INFORMAL ENGLISH: Walking to school today?
STANDARD ENGLISH: Are you walking to school today?

INFORMAL: Back by 4 this afternoon.
STANDARD: I'll be back by 4 this afternoon.

In the following pages, you will learn why, in many circumstances, the informal sentences in these examples cannot be used in place of the formal versions.

When in doubt, always choose Standard English.

More and more people are using text messages to communicate with friends, family, and coworkers. Everyone agrees that texting is very convenient. However, not everyone agrees that the informal English often used in texting is acceptable in all circumstances. A logical solution is that if you are texting friends, you can use an informal tone. However, if you are texting with your teacher, supervisor, or employer in any work- or school-related situation, choose Standard English. Even though you are texting and not writing a formal report, you are being judged. Correct grammar, spelling, word choice, and all the rest are not a choice; they are a necessity. This is a five-star recommendation!

How Can You Recognize
a Standard English Sentence?

Consider this sentence:

My music teacher performs a new song every Saturday.

This Standard English sentence includes:

- a *subject*

    My music teacher

The subject is *teacher*. To find the subject, you ask, "Who or what is this sentence about?" The answer is the teacher.

- an *action word (verb)*

    My music teacher performs.

What action does the teacher take? What does he or she do? In this sentence, the teacher gives something. The action word is *gives*.

- sometimes an *object*

    My music teacher performs a new song every Monday.

What does the teacher give? The teacher gives a quiz. *Quiz* is the object; it completes the idea of giving by telling what the teacher gave.

```
                          subject    action        object
                             |         |             |
COMPLETE SENTENCE:   My music teacher performs a new song every Monday.
```

Not all sentences contain objects. You can write a complete sentence without an object. For example, the following sentence has no object:

My music teacher sings.

Who is the sentence about (the subject)? The answer is the *teacher*. What action does the teacher take? The teacher *sings*.

Does this sentence need an object to be complete? No. The meaning is complete without another word. It is complete with just a subject (*teacher*) and a verb (*sings*).

Read the following sentences. Do they contain objects?

Marielle ate.

Mike reads fast.

The bird soars.

The newborns cry.

Bobby scored.

Each of the sentences has a subject—*Marielle, Mike, bird, newborns, Bobby*—and an action verb—*ate, reads, soars, cry, scored*—but no object. Still, they are complete thoughts and easily understood.

 ## Practice 1.1

All of the sentences in Practice 1.1 are complete thoughts. Some of the sentences contain objects; some do not. If the sentence contains an object, enter the name of the object. If the sentence does not contain an object, do not add anything. Remember, to find the object, first find the verb and ask, "What?" The first sentence is done for you.

1. I bought a book.   <u>book</u>

   Ask yourself, "What did I buy?" The answer is a book, so book *is the object.*

2. A baseball smashed the window. _____

3. I write too fast. _____

4. Jimmy drives a small truck. _____

5. You can build a sentence correctly. _____

6. The child has chickenpox. _____

7. The bank closed a branch. _____

8. The audience cheered. _____

9. A young pony galloped. _____

10. Mario sent a postcard. _____

You have successfully identified subjects, verbs, and objects in complete sentences. Are you ready for a challenge?

 Practice 1.2

Can you correct these incomplete sentences? For each incomplete sentence, add a subject, verb, or both to correct the error. The first sentence is corrected for you.

1. The wasp flying around the deck.

   The wasp flying around the deck stung Benny.

   The subject is wasp; *the missing verb is* stung.

2. Because sharks were seen close to the shore.

   _____

3. After packing the car and making lunch for the trip.

   _____

4. Before you arrived and I called the school to find you.

   _____

5. Peanut butter and jelly on white bread every day.

   _____

6. Kentucky hosting the Derby.

   _____

7. The tiny dog standing guard and yelping.

   _____

8. When your mother called the doctor.

   _____

9. After we finished dinner.

_____

_____

10. In the dark, a menacing figure walking behind me.

_____

_____

Introducing Linking Verbs

Look back at Practice 1.1. You can see that all of the sentences contain action verbs: _galloped_, _closed_, _smashed_, _drives_, and so forth. Another way to build an English sentence is with a _non-action or state-of-being_ verb. You won't find an action word (verb) such as _gives_, _walks_, or _laughs_ in this kind of sentence. However, you will find a word (a linking verb) that links two words in the sentence.

EXAMPLE: My math teacher is Mr. Albeniz.

Again, the sentence includes:

• a subject

    My math teacher

The subject, or what the sentence is about, is still the word _teacher_.

• a verb

    My math teacher is

The linking verb _is_ links the subject (_teacher_) to his name (_Mr. Albeniz_). _Teacher_ and _Mr. Albeniz_ are the same person.

Try another example:

    My computer is slow.

In this sentence, the subject is _computer_. The linking verb is _is_. What two words does the linking verb bring together? _Is_ links _computer_ with a word that describes it: _slow_.

How is this different from the first example? In the first example, _Mr. Albeniz_ equals the subject, _teacher_. In the second example, _slow_ describes the subject, _computer_.

Chapter 2 contains more information about linking verbs. For now, use this short list of linking verbs as you complete Practice 1.3: is, are, was, were, am.

Practice 1.3

In the following sentences, identify each linking verb and specify which two words the verb links. The first sentence is done for you.

1. My Aunt Hattie is a great cook.   *is* links *Aunt Hattie* and *cook*

2. Lisa, Miguel, and Dennis are best friends. _____

3. I am happy to have a few good friends. _____

   Hint: A linking verb can link the subject with a feeling or state of being.

4. The Cape was our best vacation ever. _____

5. Our two dogs were the winners! _____

   Hint: Look for the linking verb.

Where Did I Go Wrong?

If a sentence does not contain all the necessary information, a reader will have questions that can't be answered. Both subject and verb are essential elements. Without one or the other or both, the sentence seems to end too soon. Read about incomplete sentences in the next section.

Incomplete Subjects

As you read in the "Choose Standard English" section, complete sentences have certain elements in common: a subject and a verb. Sometimes, however, a word that sounds like a subject is followed by an action word or verb, but the words do not form a complete sentence. How can that be? As you read the two examples that follow, ask yourself what is missing.

   When I do more aerobic exercise.

What happens? The sentence contains an incomplete thought. A possible completion is this: When I do more aerobic exercise, feel healthier.

   After the concert is over.

What will you do after the concert? Where will you go? Here is a possible way to complete the sentence: After the concert is over, let's go out for dinner.

Are You Confused?

If you read a sentence and can't decide if it is a complete sentence, say it out loud. You may hear the error.

Incomplete Sentences with Linking Verbs

A group of words may include a word that sounds like a subject plus a linking word (verb) and still not be a complete sentence. Here are two examples:

Before a mistake is made.

What should you do? Here is one way to complete the sentence: Before a mistake is made, I'll check with you.

Because the courses I want are filled.

What will happen? You could complete the sentence this way: Because the courses I want are filled, I'll have to go to summer school.

Certain Words Tend to Make Sentences Incomplete

Certain missteps are common. For example, when you write a sentence that starts with one of the following words, be careful:

before   when   because   since   as soon as

Make sure the thought that follows is complete.

As soon as I organize my computer files.

What will happen? A possible completion is this: As soon as I organize my computer files, I'll be ready to start the new report.

Just in case you got lost in the discussion concerning elements of a sentence, let's review. If you understand this, you are way ahead!

Start by finding the subject in each of these complete sentences. Some of the sentences start with *before, when, because, since, before,* or *as soon as.* Others do not. In sentences that start with those words, look for the subject in the portion of the sentence that does *not* include those words.

EXAMPLE: Before we started high school, Mr. Neri took us on a tour of the building.

What is the subject of the sentence? If you follow the directions, you know that the subject is not in the part of the sentence that starts with *Before*. Read past the comma. You find that the sentence is about what Mr. Neri did. Mr. Neri is the subject of the sentence.

 ## Practice 1.4

*First, fill in the blank with the subject of each sentence. Then locate the verb that goes with the subject and write it next to the subject. Over the verb, indicate whether it is **AV** (for action verb) or **LV** (for linking verb). The first sentence is done for you.*

LV   Subject

|

1. Because your train arrived early, I was late picking you up. ___I was (LV)___

2. When we planned the party, you volunteered as barbecue chef.

   _____

3. Jack staggered to the door. _____

4. Kelly is my youngest child. _____

5. Since he started baking for the holidays, my husband has used 10 pounds of sugar! _____

6. Although Kathy was exhausted, she drove home from work and started making dinner. _____

7. Our dog always greets me at the door. _____

8. Before Ted eats breakfast, he likes to run or walk a few miles.

   _____

9. As soon as Ted finishes his run, his day begins. _____

10. Many parts of the country have had more rain this year than before.

    _____

Check your answers in the Answer Key.

Starting Sentences with *-ing* Verbs

Another misstep can occur when you start a sentence with an *-ing* verb. (Grammarians call these *participles*.)

EXAMPLE: Flying through the air gracefully.

Flying is the participle.

This is not a complete thought. An action is taking place (flying), but who did it? The subject is missing. Here is a possible completion: The eagle was flying through the air gracefully. The subject is *eagle*, and the verb is *was flying*.

Here is another possible completion: Flying through the air gracefully, the eagle suddenly swooped to the ground. The subject is *eagle*, and the verb is *swooped*.

Try another example:

Crunching potato chips and pretzels all through the movie.

What seems to be the action? *Crunching* is clearly the activity. However, is this example a complete sentence? If not, what is missing? If you wondered who was doing the crunching, you were on the right track. This group of words (it's not a sentence) does not contain a subject. How can you add a subject to the sentence?

Here are three solutions that add a subject to complete the sentence. For each sentence, the subject and the verb are labeled:

```
       subject     verb
          |          |
       I was crunching potato chips and pretzels all through the movie.
```

```
       subject           verb
       ┌──┴──┐             |
    My friends were crunching potato chips and pretzels all through the movie.
```

```
              subject               verb
                 |                    |
    All through the movie, we annoyed people by crunching potato chips and pretzels.
```

Practice 1.5

In this practice, some sentences are complete thoughts. Others are not. Look for participle problems and make the necessary corrections. If the sentence is correct, let it remain as it is. The first one is done for you.

1. Flying in a very large passenger jet.

   Flying in a very large passenger jet has been a goal of mine for a long time.

2. Landing on his feet.

_____

3. Trying hard to pass the driver's test.

_____

4. We were expecting rainy weather.

_____

5. Taking the trip to Walt Disney World.

_____

6. I earned a free room by encouraging my friends to go along.

_____

7. Graduating from the computer program.

_____

8. Working to earn money for college.

_____

9. Steering my car around the pothole.

_____

10. Having a day off when it snows is such a great surprise!

_____

 ## Practice 1.6

Let's try this once more. In the following sentences, identify the subject and the verb. Write AV _over the action verb or_ LV _over the linking verb. Remember that an action verb does exactly what you would expect it to do. It expresses some sort of "doing." Examples include_ hit, leap, drive, laugh, shout. _A linking verb does not express action; however, it can connect one word in the sentence to another._

                                LV

                                 |

EXAMPLE: My son's <u>guitar</u> is a Gibson.

The verb, is, _links the subject,_ guitar, _to its name,_ Gibson.

1. Food prices rose 5 percent.

2. These vegetables are organic.

3. Because we both hate the cold, we need warmer weather for camping.

4. The puppy barked incessantly.

5. As soon as the food arrives, we will eat.

6. When I spoke to you a week ago, you were very sick.

7. These apples are McIntoshes.

8. After we eat dinner, we can take a long walk.

9. Our dog is a 20-pound whippet.

10. She races across a field just the way a greyhound would.

Check your answers in the Answer Key before you go on to the next section.

 Run-On Sentences

A complete sentence is good; many complete sentences running together are not. The latter are called run-on sentences. Sentences that run together with commas are called comma faults. Consider this run-on sentence:

We've lost sight of many civilizations their monuments still stand.

The two thoughts in this sentence are the following:

We've lost sight of many civilizations.

Their monuments still stand.

In a later chapter, you will learn more about correcting sentence errors with punctuation. Consider the following sentence:

You can also correct the a run-on sentence error by adding a word or two:

We've lost sight of many civilizations; their monuments still stand.

In this sentence, the two complete thoughts are connected by a semicolon.

We've lost sight of many civilizations, yet their monuments still stand.

In this second version, the sentences are combined with a comma plus *yet*.

Practice 1.7

Find the run-on sentences in this exercise and correct those sentences. If a sentence is correct, leave it as it is.

1. What is a run-on sentence I need to stop writing them.

   _____

2. In our solar system we have eight planets, I can name all of them.

   _____

3. I looked through Aidan's telescope I saw Saturn's rings.

   _____

4. It's noon be sure to wear sun block.

   _____

5. I kept looking at her she never said hello.

   _____

Comma Fault

Read the following sentence:

> We've lost sight of many civilizations, their monuments still stand, we should try to study those civilizations.

How many thoughts are run together in this last sentence? The sentence has three thoughts.

> We've lost sight of many civilizations.
> Their monuments still stand.
> We should try to study those civilizations.

You can correct the comma fault error by ending complete thoughts in one of the following ways. First, a complete sentence can end with a period:

> Although we've lost sight of many civilizations, their monuments still stand. We should try to study those civilizations.

Second, two complete thoughts can be joined with a semicolon:

> We've lost sight of many civilizations even though their monuments still stand; we should try to study those civilizations.

Practice 1.8

Find the comma fault errors in these sentences and correct them.

1. Carlos is a skilled carpenter, he built his own home.

   _____

2. It rained for three days, I almost canceled the camping trip.

   _____

3. Some athletes believe a jump rope is the best exercise, they think it is the best exercise for conditioning your body for sports.

   _____

4. First put flour in the bowl, follow this with the sugar, finish with a pinch of salt.

   _____

5. Last summer I learned to surf, I never thought I'd be able to.

   _____

Practice 1.9

In this exercise, you will find incomplete sentences, run-on sentences, and comma faults. Correct the errors and check your answers with those in the Answer Key.

1. I had so much to do today, and we had a department meeting, and I organized my desk first.

   _____

2. Organizing the office and my desk.

   _____

3. Washington Irving is known as the father of the American short story he wrote "Rip Van Winkle" and "The Legend of Sleepy Hollow."

   _____

4. As soon as he woke up.

   _____

5. Because we've never met.

_____

6. The president had a busy day he gave a major speech then he led a discussion of the issues.

_____

7. I'll expect you at 9 a.m. we'll have a meeting Abby will join us at 3 p.m.

_____

8. Whenever you get up in the morning.

_____

9. Call me, I'll be waiting in the office, I won't leave until I hear from you.

_____

10. He arrived wearing a heavy coat and it was 80 degrees and the sun was so hot.

_____

Building Complex Sentences

What makes sentences more complex? More complex sentences have variations on the simple subject and action or linking verb. One variation is a *compound subject* (more than one subject). In "I packed the car," the subject is *I*. In "Jack packed the car," the subject is *Jack*. But the following example has a compound subject.

　　　Jack and I packed the car.

Here, the compound subject is *Jack and I.*

When a compound subject includes the person writing or speaking, always mention the other person first. Never say, "me and Jack." Read more about this in Chapter 6, "Pronouns."

A second variation is a compound action verb. Instead of two simple sentences, such as "I ate the whole cake" and "I finished the cookies, too," these thoughts could be combined into one sentence with a compound action verb:

　　　I ate the whole cake and finished the cookies, too.

The compound action verb is *ate* and *finished*. In the same way, "We filled the gas tank" and "We checked the tires as well" could be combined into a complex sentence:

> We filled the gas tank and checked the tires.

Practice 1.10

Find the compound subject or verb in each sentence. Underline the subject once and place the verb in parentheses. Two of the sentences have both compound subjects and verbs.

1. Jack and Harry drive much too fast.

2. I won't drive or travel with either of them.

3. Minnie and Maxie, our two kittens, are very mischievous.

4. You and I will make the posters and hang them up.

5. Mike and Jose, who are single parents and students, study or socialize every night.

Before you take another step forward, think about this: You've seen that verbs can show action or can link one part of a sentence to another. They have a name—*verb*—but they also have a job—to show action or link words in a sentence. We can say the same thing about other words as well. For example, the *subject* of a sentence tells us what the sentence talks about. That is its job. But what is its *name*?

The name for a subject can be either of two parts of speech: *noun* or *pronoun*. A noun is a person, place, or thing. A pronoun is simply a word that stands in for a noun. Look at the following pair of sentences. In the second sentence, what might *she* stand in for?

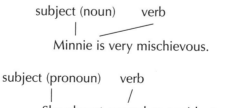

If you said that *She* stands in for *Minnie*, you are right. You will learn about pronouns in Chapter 6.

Practice 1.11

For each sentence, identify the underlined word (noun/pronoun or verb) and its job (subject or action/linking word).

1. The <u>truck</u> stopped at a red light. _____

2. A large rock <u>hit</u> the windshield. _____

3. Our car <u>is</u> old. _____

4. <u>It</u> makes terrible noises. _____

5. Irene <u>was</u> late for work. _____

6. <u>She</u> stayed late to finish her work. _____

7. <u>Mack</u> immediately called for a tow truck. _____

8. The child <u>fell</u> from the swing. _____

9. <u>Betsy and David</u> decided to put off the discussion until the morning.

_____

10. <u>They</u> heaved a sigh of relief. _____

2

More About Subjects, Action Verbs, and Linking Verbs

You've learned to recognize subjects and verbs in sentences. Now you will see that subjects and verbs relate to each other in a special way.

Subject and Verb Agreements

Subjects and verbs have a special relationship. We say that a verb "agrees" with the subject in number. Another way to refer to number is to say "singular" (one) or "plural" (more than one). In the following sentence, the subject, *bird*, is singular. Because the subject is singular, the verb ends in *-s*.

subject   verb

A bird sits on my windowsill.

Bird is the subject; *sits* is the action verb.

In the next example, the subject, *birds*, is plural. Because the subject is plural, the verb does not end in *-s*.

subject   verb

Two birds sit on my windowsill.

As you read previously, the verb does not end in *-s*. That might not sound logical. Everyone knows that an *s* means plural! In fact, that is true for most nouns such as the noun *birds* but not for verbs.

17

Verbs Ending in -s Are Not Plural

A singular subject (for example, *bird*) is usually followed by an action verb that ends in -s (*sits*). It's true that we think of the addition of *s* as plural, but that's not true when it comes to action verbs.

singular subject   singular action verb

An energetic teenager sweeps my deck every spring.

Practice 2.1

Choose the correct verb form in each sentence.

1. The recipe (list/lists) flour and sugar among the ingredients.

2. Kareem and I (drink/drinks) coffee together every morning.

3. Jorge and his sister (posts/post) a new video each week.

4. One customer on Gino's list (need/needs) a new truck.

5. Savings accounts in the two banks (pay/pays) different interest rates.

6. In Phoenix, Arizona, the sun (shine/shines) almost every day.

7. My friends and I (meet/meets) every Thursday to review for the Friday math quiz.

8. Connecticut, Rhode Island, and Massachusetts (is/are) New England states.

9. Nuclear weapons (is/are) still a threat to the world.

10. Your choice of Standard English (is/are) always a safe one.

Plural Verbs Do Not End in -s

A verb that agrees with a plural subject is written without an -s. Although it may seem strange, it's true.

plural subject   plural verb

About 100 meteorites hit the earth each year.

Practice 2.2

Choose the correct verb form in each sentence.

1. The spring flowers (sits/sit) in a vase.

2. When they spend too much time over coffee, they (takes/take) the chance of being late for work.

3. My children, Josh and Emily, always (skip/skips) that part of the task.

4. Sharpened pencils and crisp white paper (sits/sit) on the desk.

5. Employees and their boss (eats/eat) in the cafeteria.

6. Sam and his friends (shares/share) the cost of gasoline.

7. Meteorites of various sizes (fall/falls) to earth without hurting us.

8. Groups of bright flowers and stepping stones (creates/create) a colorful garden.

9. Two squirrels (gathers/gather) acorns in my yard.

10. That government agency (lead/leads) the fight to eliminate hunger.

Irregular Plurals

You are used to reading plural subjects that end in *-s*, as in *flowers*, *pencils*, and *employees*. Occasionally, though, words form their plurals in an irregular way. For example, what is the plural of *child*? That would be *children*; there is no *-s* in sight. Look at the following list for other examples of plural nouns that do not end in *-s*. You'll find more about plurals in Chapter 11, "Spelling."

Singular	Plural
woman	women
tooth	teeth
man	men
mouse	mice
cactus	cacti

Linking Verbs Also Have Singular and Plural Forms

In the previous exercise, all of the sentences contain action verbs: *sit, take, eat.* However, linking verbs also have singular and plural forms. Some of them, such as *is* (a form of the verb *to be*), change their spelling completely in order to agree with the subject. Later in this chapter, study the list of *to be* verbs in the present, past, and future time.

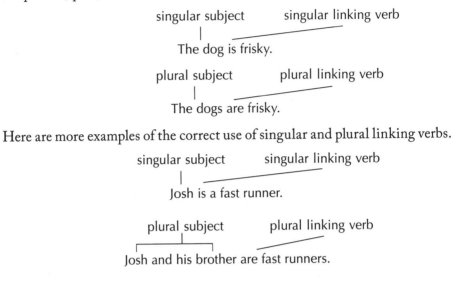

singular subject   singular linking verb

The dog is frisky.

plural subject   plural linking verb

The dogs are frisky.

Here are more examples of the correct use of singular and plural linking verbs.

singular subject   singular linking verb

Josh is a fast runner.

plural subject   plural linking verb

Josh and his brother are fast runners.

Subject and Verbs Agree Even When Separated

Agreement between subject and verb exists even when a phrase comes between the two. When you search for the subject of a sentence, beware of interrupting phrases.

INCORRECT: The mayor unlike his assistants are going to prison for fraud.

In the previous sentence, *unlike his assistants* is an interrupting phrase. Certain words, including *unlike his assistants* make us think the subject is plural even though it isn't. Of course, that is because the phrase comes between the singular subject, *mayor*, and the verb. The singular subject requires a singular verb.

In contrast, look at the difference when you substitute the word *and* for the interrupting phrase:

plural subject   plural verb

CORRECT: The mayor and his assistants are going to prison for fraud.

In the previous sentence, *and* makes the subject plural (*Mayor* and *assistants*). The plural subject needs a plural verb, *are*.

Prepositions and Prepositional Phrases

In Chapter 4, you will learn about interrupting phrases that start with prepositions. A preposition is a connecting word that shows a relationship between a noun and some other word in the sentence.

> We put the dog in the doghouse.

The preposition *in* shows the relationship between the dog and the doghouse.

Prepositional phrases are a major reason for missteps because they often come between the subject and verb. Here is an example of an incorrect sentence. The subject and verb do not agree.

```
  subject      prepositional phrase   verb
    |                   |               |
```
A garden (with so many vegetables) are hard to keep watered.

To fix the mistake, ask yourself these questions:

- What is the subject? The subject is *garden*.

- Is *garden* singular or plural? It is singular.

- According to what you've learned so far, should the verb be singular or plural? It should be singular.

- What is the verb in the sentence? The verb is *are*.

- Is the word *are* singular or plural? It's plural. The singular form of the verb *are* is the word *is*.

Now you know why the subject and verb disagree.

Here is one way to correct the sentence:

> A garden with so many vegetables is hard to keep watered.

Practice 2.3

In each of the following sentences, find the subject. Choose the verb that agrees in number. Don't be fooled by interrupting phrases.

1. The dog and cat (is/are) good company for each other.

2. The chair and the table in the attic (is/are) too big for the space.

3. Alex and Maria (runs/run) to work each morning.

4. Kim and her friend (is/are) at the conference.

5. One of the ATMs (is/are) out of order.

6. The first peach pie of the summer (taste/tastes) delicious.

7. He and his classmates (appear/appears) so much taller than last year.

8. Nothing in all the rooms of this building (is/are) new.

9. One of the packages (are/is) open.

10. The child with all the dogs (walk/walks) in the park every day.

11. The car with many people in the back (are/is) going much too fast.

12. The boys in the green and white jerseys (play/plays) for our school.

13. The uniforms for teams such as mine (changes/change) every few years.

14. Each of my sisters (are/is) helpful to me when I don't understand my homework.

15. The information in these blogs (is/are) not necessarily true.

Using Linking Verbs

As you've learned, a verb does one of two things: Either it shows the subject's action, or it links the subject to a descriptive word. See what the verb does in each of the following examples.

```
subject     action verb
   |             |
The 18-wheeler swerved.
```

In this example, *swerved* states the subject's action. If you close your eyes, you can visualize the action in the sentence.

```
subject       linking verb
   |              /
The 18-wheeler is huge.
```

In this sentence, the verb *is* does not provide a picture of an action. Instead, it connects or links the descriptive word (*huge*) to the subject (*18-wheeler*). The description happens because this sentence uses a linking word.

Verbs also show time. That is true of both action and linking verbs.

subject   action verb (present)

My friend drives more than 15,000 miles a year.

subject   action verb (past)

My friend drove more than 3,000 miles.

subject   action verb (future)

My friend will drive as few miles as possible next year.

subject   linking verb (present)

The store is open.

subject   linking verb (past)

The store was open.

subject   linking verb (future)

The store will be open.

Linking verbs *is*, *was*, and *will be* are all part of a large category of words called *to be* (non-action or state-of-being) *verbs*. *To be* verbs are used in present time, past time, and future time as well as other times you'll learn about later in the book.

 ## *To Be* Agrees with the Subject

Simple present, past, and future forms of *to be* change according to the singular or plural subject of the sentence. The following sentences show which form of *to be* is correct in each situation. The subjects are all *pronouns*, words that stand in for nouns.

Present Time

I am first.

You (or we) are second.

He (or she or it) is third.

They are last.

Past Time

I was first.

You (or we) were third.

He (or she or it) was second.

They were last.

Future Time

I will be first.

You will be second.

He will be third.

They will be last.

Be is a unique verb in that it can combine with helping words to form a slightly different meaning. See how *would, could, should, to, can,* and *will* combine with *be*.

 Practice 2.4

Combine one of the helping words—would, could, should, ought to, can, will—with be *to finish each of the following sentences. More than one helping word may be correct.*

1. You _____ my best friend!

2. Our family _____ ready at noon for the picnic.

3. My grandfather _____ more careful when he walks down the ice-covered stairs.

4. Last year's champion _____ expected to take first place again this year.

5. You're expected _____ at the finish line.

6. You _____ so proud of your son's award.

7. We _____ expecting you on Sunday for lunch.

8. I _____ a much better violinist if I practiced more.

9. Sunshine and warm temperatures _____ expected for the weekend.

10. My entire class _____ at the end-of-year picnic.

 Linking verbs are often verbs of the senses. Common linking verbs include the following:

am	appear	are	be	become
feel	grow	is	look	seem
smell	sound	taste	was	were

 ## Practice 2.5

Choose a linking verb to complete each sentence.

1. The new mother cried, "I (are, am) so tired after being up all night!"

2. The strawberries (seem, seems) to be fine after the freeze.

3. The muffin (taste, tastes) delicious.

4. We (was, were) expected at 9 a.m.; we arrived at 11.

5. The room (grew/grows) quiet as we entered.

6. The weather (look, looks) fine to me.

7. We—my friend and I—(was/were) so embarrassed.

8. Every time we go camping, the weather (become/becomes) cold and cloudy.

9. The berries (taste/tastes) delicious and are so good for you.

10. The new paint (is, are) so much brighter.

 ## Practice 2.6

Identify the subject in each sentence, and determine whether it is singular or plural. Then choose the action or linking verb that agrees with it. The first one is done for you.

1. <u>Bob and Julie</u> (play/plays) board games with their children. ___plural/play___

2. Juan (play/plays) board games with his children, too. _____

3. After the soccer game, my brother (was/were) tired. _____

4. Ten dancers in the video suddenly (stops/stop) moving. _____

5. In that movie, all the characters (appears/appear) bored. _____

6. Summer flowers (smell/smells) so fragrant. _____

7. The marching band (sound/sounds) loud and brassy. _____

8. The teacher said, "That child (looks/look) very ill." _____

9. Our team always (race/races) to the finish line. _____

10. A tall, wooden fence (protects/protect) the property. _____

Linking Verb Combinations

Linking verbs have two more talents.

- They can be combined with other words, e.g., *here + is = here's*.
- They can be combined with *not*. For example, *is + not = isn't*. As you can see, however, to combine them, you must drop a letter or letters to make room for an apostrophe. All of these combinations are called *contractions*.

Here are some examples of the first kind of combination.

we are = we're

they are = they're

there is = there's

here is = here's

you are = you're

it is = it's

she is = she's

Avoid the common error of confusing *it's* with *its*. Without the apostrophe, *its* indicates possession.

For a very long time, the cat seemed happy to chase *its* tail.

Note: The cat owns the tail.

Here are some examples of "not" combinations:

is + not = isn't

are + not = aren't

was + not = wasn't

were + not = weren't

 Practice 2.7

In each sentence, change the two words in the parentheses to a contraction.

1. (Here is) my plan for the trip. _____

2. (Is not) this a perfect day to get started? _____

3. (She is) the best person for the job. _____

4. (There is) only one correct answer. _____

5. (They are) taking their time. _____

6. You (are not) ready yet! _____

7. The cake (was not) ready to come out of the oven. _____

8. (Were not) you going to call me? _____

9. (There is) only one pillow left for three people. (That is) a problem.
_____

10. (Was not) today your day to open the office? _____

 Practice 2.8

Use everything you've learned in this chapter to choose the word that correctly completes each sentence.

1. The boy and his friend (is/are) on the same baseball team.

2. She and Emmy (is/are) at the music competition.

3. The jars in the carton (is/are) eight ounces each.

4. The chocolate cupcake more than anything else (taste/tastes) delicious.

5. In the end, they (was/were) last to get on the ride.

6. It seems that the child they brought (were/was) too short to be allowed on the ride.

7. The new friends I met last year (was/were) the best thing that happened to me.

8. The beautiful flowers in the clay pot (are/is) called geraniums.

9. Micah and Gabriel, twin brothers, (is/are) very talented 13-year-olds.

10. Teenagers who are hungry (complains/complain) until they are fed.

3

Descriptive Words

If we never used descriptive words (adjectives and adverbs), how boring would our writing and speaking be? Look at the following sentence to see how descriptive words (adjectives) add color and meaning to sentences.

adjective   noun   adjective   noun   noun (subject)   adjective
   | | \ | | /
As stormy clouds hovered above the bleak landscape, I felt uneasy.

Adjectives in this sentence most definitely add color and meaning. You can picture "stormy clouds" hovering just above a "bleak landscape" and can imagine how these features lead to a feeling of uneasiness.

Extra credit: Think back to the discussion of linking verbs. How does the word *uneasy* function as an adjective (descriptive word) in this sentence? The linking verb, *felt*, links I to *uneasy*.

 ## In the Know About Adjectives

Adjectives describe nouns (names of people, places, or things) and pronouns (words that stand in for nouns). Here are two examples:

adj.   noun   adj.
 | | |
A narrow alley separates tall two houses.

pronoun   adj.   adj.
  | / |
She is older by only five minutes.

The words *a*, *an*, and *the* function as adjectives (also called articles). They add meaning by pointing to nouns, as the following examples show:

(article)   adj.   noun

I am working on a long report for my history class.

article   noun

An icicle formed on the roof.

Note: *An* describes a noun that starts with a vowel (a, e, i, o, u, y).

Adjectives and Where to Put Them

All languages have their particular ways of placing words in sentences. In some languages, such as English, an adjective usually appears before the noun.

adjective   noun

The injured quarterback played only one quarter of the game.

In other languages, such as Spanish, adjectives are most often, but not always, placed after the noun. Here is the same sentence in Spanish and English. In Spanish, the adjective (*Espanola*) follows the noun, (*mujer*).

La mujer Espanola esta qui. (The Spanish woman is here.)

Adjectives Describe Nouns and Pronouns

An adjective is most often—but not always—placed in front of the noun or pronoun it describes.

adjective noun adjective noun

My old sink has a leaky faucet.

You can be so creative with the English language! You can even use nouns as adjectives. Look at the following phrases. The first word in each phrase is an adjective that was created from a noun.

adjective

California peaches

race horse

war movie

shoe store

When you use a noun as an adjective, the adjective always comes before the noun, and it's most often singular. For example, you may buy shoes at more than one store, but the word is never *shoes* stores.

Adjectives Follow Linking Verbs

Adjectives follow linking verbs and describe the subject (noun or pronoun) of the sentence.

subject pronoun   LV   adjectives

He is cold and forbidding.

In this sentence, the adjectives *cold* and *forbidding* tell us more about (describe) the pronoun *he*. The verb *is* links the adjectives to the subject pronoun *he*.

Practice 3.1

Check your skill in recognizing adjectives. Some describe nouns. Other adjectives follow linking words and describe the subject, which is also a noun. In the following sentences, identify each adjective and the word it describes.

	Adjective(s)	Word Described
1. My new neighbor owns an old dog.	_____	_____
2. The floppy-eared dog is slow and gentle.	_____	_____
3. A heavy snow ruined our plans.	_____	_____
4. The decaying tooth is painful.	_____	_____
5. Aidan, tired and cranky, walked out of the room.	_____	_____
6. Washington State apples are crisp and delicious.	_____	_____

7. Three hungry children finished a large plate of spaghetti. (Hint: Two words describe children.) _____   _____

8. Lincoln was steadfast during the Civil War. _____   _____

9. The generous woman brought bags of food to the meeting. _____   _____

10. Manuel has a brilliant smile. _____   _____

Two Adjectives Are Usually Separated by a Comma

When two adjectives describe a noun, the adjectives are usually separated by a comma.

adjective   adjective

| |

All the rusty, dangerous metal had to be removed from the yard.

Two Adjectives Separated by *And*

If two adjectives describe the noun and if the word *and* can logically be placed between them, then insert commas before and after the adjectives. Notice in the following examples how this writing technique puts emphasis on the adjectives.

noun   adjectives

A storm, icy and wet, blanketed the Northeast.

noun   adjectives

My children, tan and healthy, returned from day camp.

As you complete the following practice exercise, you need to remember when to add a comma:

- Add a comma if the sentence still makes sense when the adjectives are written in reverse order.

- Add a comma if the sentence would make sense with an *and* between the adjectives.

Here are examples of adjectives that require a comma. You can reverse them, and they still make sense.

bright, happy smile
powerful, abusive leader

The following phrases do not require commas because if you reverse the adjectives, they won't still make sense.

red brick house
black wool skirt

Practice 3.2

Place commas where they are needed in these sentences. Not all the sentences require commas.

1. Casey is an easygoing lovable dog.

2. Mike and I learned how to use the new app.

3. A heavy bulky box arrived at our front door.

4. Her tall dark handsome date arrived exactly on time.

5. We streamed a gory, tension-filled horror movie.

6. The gooey caramel candy stuck to my fingers.

7. Ricardo gave me a creative usable suggestion.

8. Four hungry tired children arrived for lunch.

9. A violent loud storm scared the audience.

10. A repeated high-pitched tapping noise annoyed us.

Adjectives Used to Express Comparisons

Adjectives can be used to express comparisons. In that case, a simple spelling change occurs. Notice the addition of either *-er* or *-est* to the end of the adjective.

My car is new.

Your car is newer.

Her car is the newest of the three.

To compare one car with another, you add *-er* (newer). To compare more than two cars, add *-est*. To compare one car with all others in a group, add *-er*.

> My car is newer than any other on our block.

You can also use the words *more* and *most* to compare adjectives. *More* compares two things while *most* compares three or more.

> Football is a more physical sport than fishing. (Two sports are compared.)

> Apple pie is the most delicious dessert of all. (All desserts are compared to apple pie.)

Caution: Don't combine *more* with an adjective ending in *-er* or *-est*.

INCORRECT: My office is more brighter than yours.
CORRECT: My office is brighter than yours.

INCORRECT: My office is the most brightest in the building.
CORRECT: My office is the brightest in the building.

Spelling Changes for Comparison Adjectives

The spelling of some adjectives changes completely for comparisons.

ADJECTIVE	COMPARISON OF TWO	COMPARISON OF MORE THAN TWO
good	better	best
much	more	most
little (amount)	less	least
little or small (size)	smaller	smallest

Remember that the spelling of the adjective depends upon whether you are comparing one, two, or more things. For example, one car is large; of two cars, this one is larger; of three or more cars, this one is the largest.

Practice 3.3

Look for errors in comparison. Correct the errors.

1. My car is newer than the three of yours. _____

2. Chris is the better gymnast in the class. _____

3. Her classroom is littler than yours. _____

4. This room is the most brightest of all. _____

5. That pond is the most shallowest of any in this area. _____

6. That fish is the most largest in the pond. _____

7. Aldo's story is the longer of any in the class. _____

8. That is the story of the wisest man. _____

9. Did you foolishly want to be the most silliest person in the class?

_____

10. Our new dog is the most tallest of any I've ever seen. _____

_____

 Were you confused by sentences 4, 6, 9, and 10? Avoid this common error with comparison of adjectives. These sentences complicate the -er, -est choice by incorrectly adding the word *more* or the word *most* to the sentence. The following two sentences are also incorrect:

INCORRECT: Solomon is the most wisest man I know.
INCORRECT: Solomon is the more wisest man I know.

Simple is correct:
CORRECT: Solomon is the wisest man I know.

Pronouns That Function as Adjectives

Think about this earlier example: *My old sink has a leaky faucet.* In the phrase *my old sink*, *sink* is clearly the subject of the sentence and a noun. *My* and *old* describe *sink*. Did you recognize *my* as a pronoun? It is one, but it has a special function here: It functions as an adjective describing the sink (showing who owns it).

Pronouns can function in three main ways. The following chart displays these functions. You will find this chart very useful as you progress through the book.

Pronouns

SUBJECT PRONOUNS	OBJECT PRONOUNS (RECEIVE THE ACTION)	OWNERSHIP PRONOUNS
I	me	my, mine
you	you	your, yours
he	him	his
she	her	her, hers
it	it	its
we	us	our, ours
they	them	their, theirs
who	whom	

Placing Adjectives with Nouns

Placing adjectives in front of nouns comes naturally to anyone whose first language is English. Would you ever think of saying this?

noun adjective
| |
My grandfather spry lives with us.

A person whose first language is English would automatically say,

adjective noun
| |
My spry grandfather lives with us.

This is not true in all languages. In Spanish, for example, certain kinds of adjectives are placed after nouns. Consider the Spanish phrase for the White House:

noun adjective
| /
la Casa Blanca

Translated word for word, this means "the House White."

Compare that with more English examples:

adjective   noun
| |
Our team has an enormous linebacker.

adjective noun

We saw the winning film.

As you read earlier in this chapter, the rule to put adjectives first changes when adjectives follow linking verbs (LVs).

noun LV adjective adjective

The weather is hot and humid.

Here the adjectives follow the verb and describe the noun that came before the linking verb. In other words, the words *hot* and *humid* describe *weather*.

Adjectives seem to get around a lot! They can appear before a noun, after a noun, or following a linking verb to link the subject and the descriptive word. Try the following exercise in order to sort out all that you've learned.

 ## Practice 3.4

Find the subject and verb in each sentence, deciding whether the verb is an action verb (such as hit*) or a linking verb (*is, was, are, *and so forth). Find any adjectives, and indicate the nouns they describe.*

1. Simple, tailored clothes are preferred. _____

2. The sale is storewide. _____

3. Mario streamed a romantic movie. _____

4. He loves adventure films. _____

5. My afternoon snack is big! _____

6. SpaceX™ designs advanced spacecraft. _____

7. Aidan and Joseph look cheerful. _____

8. They are the new students in eleventh grade. _____

9. What was your favorite video? _____

10. January and February were extremely cold. _____

Separate Two Adjectives That Describe the Same Noun

Place a comma between two adjectives that describe the same noun. The two adjectives must be of equal importance. Or, insert the word *and* between them. The sentence maintains its meaning.

> We were concerned about the rusty, dangerous metal pieces on the sidewalk.

> We were concerned about the rusty and dangerous metal pieces on the sidewalk.

You will know the comma is correct if the sentence maintains its meaning when the adjectives are reversed. In the following two sentences, for example, the meaning is basically the same.

> We were concerned about the rusty, dangerous metal pieces on the sidewalk.

> We were concerned about the dangerous, rusty metal pieces on the sidewalk.

Practice 3.5

In each sentence, insert a comma between the two adjectives where needed.

1. The pleasant older woman sat next to me.

2. The cool clear water invited us in.

3. Ms. Merrit gave us a difficult final exam.

4. I always eat sweet and juicy apples with pleasure.

5. This year, voting was so much faster because of a knowledgeable courteous team of workers.

Adjectives That Have Two or More Syllables

While the changes involving comparison of adjectives can be simple (new, newer, newest), more complicated changes are necessary for adjectives that have two or more syllables. Say the following out loud. Do your ears object to what they hear?

pleasant	pleasanter	pleasantest
thoughtful	thoughtfuler	thoughtfulest

How do you solve the problem of awkward pronunciation? Instead of making the adjectives so long, you use the words *more* and *most* to express the comparison. But be careful: As you learned earlier in this chapter, never use *more* or *most* plus *-er* or *-est*.

INCORRECT: This graphic organizer is difficulter than the one I used last time.

INCORRECT: This graphic organizer is more difficulter than the one I used last time.

CORRECT: This graphic organizer is more difficult than the one I used last time.

Here's a chart of correct comparisons:

ADJECTIVE	COMPARISON OF TWO	COMPARISON OF MORE THAN TWO
pleasant	more pleasant	most pleasant
thoughtful	more thoughtful	most thoughtful
difficult	more difficult	most difficult
interesting	more interesting	most interesting

There are exceptions to this rule of two-syllable adjectives. For example, if a two-syllable adjective ends in *-y*, drop the *y*, add an *i*, and add the *-er*, or *-est*.

happy	happier	happiest
easy	easier	easiest

 ## Practice 3.6

Insert one of these adjectives in each sentence. Change the form of the word according to the meaning of the sentence. More than one adjective may be correct for some sentences. Choose one.

profitable	speedy	difficult	ugly	appealing
tall	long	loud	high	boring

1. I've never seen a less attractive pair of shoes; they are the _____ I've ever seen!

2. Your radio is the _____ one.

3. If you begin to watch your expenditures carefully, your store will be _____ than it was before.

4. Amanda grew a lot this year; she is the _____ girl in our class.

5. Of the three children in the race, Jason finished first; he's definitely the _____.

6. I saw the _____ building in New York.

7. Everyone said this play was wonderful. I thought it was the _____ one I'd ever seen.

8. Jill is charming; she's the _____ person I know.

9. Of all the preparations for tests, this has been the _____.

10. When I'm in a hurry, I avoid River Road, because it is the _____ route to my house.

Adjectives That Take Completely Different Forms

Some adjectives take completely different forms to show comparison. For these, you need to memorize their meanings and spellings. Here are some common examples.

ADJECTIVE	COMPARISON OF TWO	COMPARISON OF MORE THAN TWO
little (amount)	less	least
little or small (size)	smaller	smallest
good	better	best
bad	worse	worst
much	more	most
many	more	most
well (healthy)	better	best
far	farther	farthest

Finally, and just as you thought you'd seen every side of adjectives, there are two more oddities you should know about. Some adjectives can correctly show comparison in two ways:

ADJECTIVE	COMPARISON OF TWO	COMPARISON OF MORE THAN TWO
simple	simpler/more simple	simplest/most simple
common	commoner/more common	commonest/most common

Some adjectives have no comparative forms because the simplest form expresses the only degree possible. The following words do not have a comparative form:

final   dead   unique   vertical   wrong

Think about it this way: You can't be *more* or *most* dead. You are simply dead. *Unique* means one of a kind. Something can't be *more* or *most* one of a kind. It is unique!

 ## Practice 3.7

Choose the correct adjective form in each sentence.

1. I feel more (comfortable/comfortabler) in these new shoes.

2. After being home sick for two weeks, Jose finally feels (good/better).

3. Kurt is considered the (shrewder/shrewdest) player in our chess club.

4. Kyle's the (better/best) of the two ball players.

5. Your artwork is (unique/more uniquer); mine is commonplace.

6. This shell is the most (common/commonest) of all.

7. This week we had the (easyest/easiest) test ever!

8. This is the (worse/worst) cold I've ever had.

9. This coffeepot makes the (baddest/worst) coffee.

10. Eric is the most (efficientest/efficient) worker of all.

 ## Practice 3.8

Correct the errors and rewrite these sentences.

1. I ate the smaller of the three piece of cake on the plate.

_____

2. A student late and unprepared interrupted the lecturer.

_____

3. My backyard contains, a huge un-mowed lawn.

   _____

4. You should be carefuller when you drive on icy roads.

   _____

5. I couldn't have found an easyer game for us to play!

   _____

6. Your solution is more unique.

   _____

7. I thought last night's homework was the worse we've had all week.

   _____

8. Your answers were good, but mine were best.

   _____

9. The older you get, the more difficulter it is to learn a foreign language.

   _____

10. A large muscular dog protected us.

    _____

4

More About Descriptive
Words and Phrases

You've learned a great deal about one kind of descriptive word—the adjective, a word that describes nouns. Now you can move on to adverbs, words that add color and meaning to a sentence by describing verbs, adjectives, and other adverbs. Learning about adverbs is not just another grammar lesson; learning about adverbs also gives a huge lift to your vocabulary.

Adverbs and How to Use Them

Adverbs modify or describe verbs, adjectives, and other adverbs. You can use adverbs to add meaning to sentences because they answer the questions when, where, how, in what manner, and to what extent.

Adverbs Describe Verbs and Adjectives

The word *adverb* itself gives a clue to one of its functions. Its prefix, *ad-*, means to or toward. An adverb "moves toward" (describes) the verb. Adverbs also describe adjectives and adverbs, as you'll see a little later. However, adjectives do not describe adverbs, and adverbs do not describe nouns or pronouns.

Adverbs answer the questions how, when, and where about the words they describe.

> Abby, a new driver, drove *slowly*. (How did she drive?)

> We're leaving for our vacation *shortly*. (When are we leaving?)

> They still live *there*. (Where do they live?)

You'll recognize most adverbs easily, because they so often end in *-ly*. In fact, for many adjectives, if you add *-ly*, you transform the adjectives into adverbs.

ADJECTIVE	ADVERB
loud	loudly
near	nearly
short	shortly
rude	rudely

 Use caution! Having an *-ly* ending does not always make a word an adverb. For example, consider these words: *motherly, friendly, lovely, lonely,* and *neighborly.* All of them are adjectives. You can tell because they describe nouns.

 ## Practice 4.1

Correctly complete each sentence with one of the following adjectives. Use each word only once.

    motherly   friendly   lovely   lonely   neighborly

1. On my street, the people are _____ and help each other out with snow removal and holiday decorations.

2. You won't be _____ in this neighborhood.

3. Is your dog _____? May I pet her?

4. I planted a _____ garden with colorful flowers.

5. Mrs. Potter shows a _____ attitude toward all children she cares for.

 ### Adverbs Also Describe Other Adverbs

Adverbs also describe adjectives, and they describe other adverbs as well. Adverbs used in these ways may not end in *-ly.*

                noun (subject) verb adverb adjective
                      |
        At 65 pounds, Sadie is a rather large dog.

The adverb *rather* (meaning quite) describes the adjective *large.*

                noun (subject) verb adverb adverb
                      |
            This week went very quickly.

The adverb *very* describes the adverb *quickly.* It tells how quickly.

Adverbs Have Comparative Forms

Adjectives and adverbs have a common characteristic. They both have comparative forms. Remember this? If you want to use the adjective *tall* to compare the heights of two people and then three people, you add -*er* and -*est*:

1. My brother is tall.

2. My sister is tall*er*.

3. I am the tall*est* of all.

You've already learned that adjectives can be compared. Examples: green, greener, greenest. You added -*er* and -*est* to the words. Now you will learn about adverbs that can do the same thing. Read the following sentence and find the two adverbs.

> My girlfriend types faster than I do; she's also the fastest at texting of anyone I know.

Faster and *fastest* are the adverbs. What do they compare? *Faster* compares another person's typing speed with mine. *Fastest* compares all those I know who text, and that would include more than one other person.

In addition to adding -*er* and -*est* to adverbs, we can use the words *more*, *most*, *less*, and *least* to express degrees of adverbs.

> He's more likely to pass geometry than I am.

> Seth is most likely to receive the math award.

> The leaves are less likely to fall until the temperature drops.

> Lila is least likely to graduate unless her attendance record improves.

Practice 4.2

Choose the adverb that correctly finishes each sentence.

1. Shelley is (more likely/most likely) to take her vacation in the winter now that her children are grown.

2. Governor Humble, of all the candidates, is (more likely/most likely) to win the election.

3. My friend runs (slower/slowest) than I do.

4. The students in this class who read the (faster/fastest) are definitely at an advantage.

5. My dog is (quieter/most quiet) than yours.

To avoid confusion in the use of adjectives and adverbs, understand the job that each one does. Once again, you need to decide what job the descriptive word will perform in a particular sentence. In the following sections, you learn how to use words correctly by knowing what job they do. That is especially true of the words *real, really, good,* and *well.*

For example, *good* is usually an adjective. (My new puppy is a *good* eater. Here, *good* describes the noun *eater.*) *Well* is the adverb form of good, so it describes an action. (My car runs *well. Well* describes the verb *runs.*) The only exception occurs when referring to someone's health. Misuses of *good* and *well* commonly occur when we're talking about someone's health. Just remember that *good* refers to your state of health and functions as an adjective after the linking verb. (I *feel* good. *Feel* is a linking verb in this sentence and requires that an adjective, *good,* follow it.)

Read four common misuses in Practice 4.3. You may already know the correct form. (Adverbs are everywhere! Look back: *Already* is an adverb that describes the verb *know.*)

Practice 4.3

Correct the errors in these sentences if you can. When you read the rest of the chapter, all will be revealed.

1. Many of our camping trips have been *real* exciting.

_____

2. I don't feel *good* today.

_____

3. My friend draws *good.*

_____

4. Melanie passed the swimming test *satisfactory.*

_____

Prepositional Phrases Work Like Adjectives and Adverbs

You now know that sentences are built on the foundation of subjects (nouns and pronouns), verbs (action and linking), and descriptive words (adjectives and adverbs). Still, English sentences don't have to remain that simple.

For example, some descriptions require more than one word—a phrase—to expand the meaning: One such phrase is called a *prepositional* phrase. A prepositional phrase is a group of words that starts with a preposition and ends with an object (a noun or pronoun). A prepositional phrase describes another word in the sentence. On page 53, you'll find a list of prepositions that introduce descriptive phrases.

In the following sentence, *into* is the preposition.

prepositional phrase
|
A contestant fell into the orchestra pit.

The phrase *into the orchestra pit* describes where the contestant fell. Like an adverb, the phrase describes a verb. Prepositional phrases work like adjectives and adverbs to expand the meanings of sentences.

When to Use an Adverb

Use an adverb to give more information about verbs, adjectives, and other adverbs. You'll find that adverbs answer the questions how, when, or where.

Does It Describe a Verb?

How do you decide when to use an adverb instead of an adjective? Ask yourself this question: Does it describe a verb?

subject   verb   adverb   adverb
| | | |
The cart lurched forward suddenly.

Both *forward* and *suddenly* are adverbs that describe the verb *lurched*. The adverb *forward* answers the question of where the cart lurched. *Suddenly* answers the question of how the cart lurched.

Practice 4.4

Find the adverb in each sentence, and identify the word it describes. You may find more than one adverb in a sentence. The first one is done for you.

1. My friend mistakenly chose the most expensive shoes and then didn't buy them.
   <u>mistakenly/chose most/expensive then/did buy</u>

2. For that reason, we rarely shop together. _____

3. Belle's shoes felt much too tight. _____

4. She couldn't comfortably continue the five-mile hike. _____

5. Our dog slept happily on his new bed. _____

6. Holding a cane, the man walked slowly and carefully. _____

7. Katelin draws quickly. _____

8. The students will undoubtedly find this class a challenge. _____

9. Her friend smiled warmly at me. _____

10. The man ran quickly toward the departing bus. _____

Does It Describe an Adjective?

An adverb that describes an adjective further strengthens the description. As an example, look at the following sentences. In the first, you learn that the subject is not only exhausted, but exceptionally so.

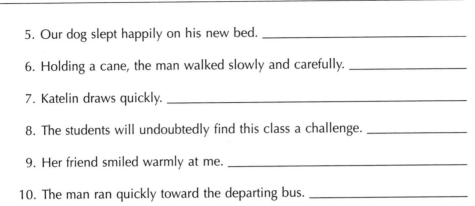

subject   verb   adv.   adjective

I was extremely exhausted.

The adverb *extremely* describes the adjective *exhausted*. *Extremely* answers the question of how much or to what degree.

subject   verb   adverb   adjective

This coffee is just warm, not hot.

The adverb *just* describes the adjective *warm*. *Just* answers the question of how much.

Practice 4.5

In each sentence, find the adverb. Note it in the adverb column. Then find the adjective it describes and note it in the column provided.

	Adverb	Word Described
1. I can see that spring will be really beautiful.	_____	_____
2. The early spring flowers are already blooming.	_____	_____

3. My deck is very dirty.   _____   _____

4. The budding tree smells so fragrant.   _____   _____

5. After a long winter, I am extremely
   grateful for spring.   _____   _____

6. Mike works too late every night.   _____   _____

7. As a result, he is always tired.   _____   _____

8. Puffy clouds drift aimlessly.   _____   _____

9. Are you absolutely sure?   _____   _____

10. My house was painted recently.   _____   _____

! Avoid a common mistake: Do not use an adjective to describe an adverb.

CORRECT: That was a really wonderful movie.
CORRECT: The cake had a wonderfully rich icing.
INCORRECT: He runs real fast.

Real is an adjective; it can't describe *fast,* an adverb.

Words That Cause Common Problems

You've learned about some words that cause common problems—*real, really, good,* and *well.* Again, if you know which words these four describe, you can make the right decision about which to use. Try this example

```
            noun        adjective
             |              |
Many of our camping trips have been exciting.
```

The sentence talks about exciting trips. If you want to emphasize the excitement, you may want to add a word to describe *exciting.* Consider the adjective *real* and the adverb *really.* Should you use an adjective to describe the adjective *exciting*? No. Adjectives describe nouns and pronouns, not other adjectives. How do you transform the adjective *real* into an adverb? Of course, you add *-ly.* Now you can use the adverb *really*:

```
     noun  verb    adverb adjective
      |     |        |       |
Many of our camping trips have been really exciting.
```

Common Adjective/Adverb Confusions

Other common words can cause the same adjective/adverb confusion—if you let them. Keep the correct use of the following words in mind as you strive for Standard English usage. Each set of words is followed by sentences in which those words are used correctly.

quick/quickly

Quick is an adjective; it describes nouns and pronouns. *Quickly* is an adverb that describes verbs.

> We took a quick trip to the beach.

Quick is an adjective that describes the noun *trip*.

> Finish your packing quickly.

Quickly is an adverb that describes the verb *finish*.

good/well

Good is an adjective, so it describes nouns and pronouns. *Good* never describes a verb. *Well* is an adverb that describes verbs. One exception: *Well* can be used as an adjective to describe someone's state of health.

> My husband is a good dancer.

Good describes the noun *dancer*.

> My husband dances well.

Well describes the verb *dances*.

> My friend Harry hasn't been well in a long time.

Well refers to Harry's state of health.

nice/nicely

Nice is an adjective, so it describes nouns and pronouns. *Nicely* is an adverb; it describes adjectives and adverbs.

> The entertainer had a nice voice.

Nice describes the noun *voice*.

> The entertainer sang nicely.

Nicely describes the verb *sang*.

Practice 4.6

Choose the correct word to finish each sentence.

1. The contestant skated so (nicely/nice)!

2. I'm a (well/good) skater, too.

3. Look (quick/quickly)! That's a shooting star.

4. It was a (really/real) good buy.

5. The bus stopped so (sudden/suddenly) that we all fell forward.

6. You can tell that Kitty doesn't feel (good/well) today.

7. She's usually such a (well/good) eater, but not today.

8. Everyone stopped to listen because she sang so (nice/nicely).

9. We can take a (quickly/quick) break before we start work this afternoon.

10. We've used our time (good/well) today.

real/really/very

Real is an adjective that describes nouns and pronouns. *Really* is an adverb that describes verbs, adjectives, and adverbs. *Very* is an adverb that describes and emphasizes adjectives and adverbs.

> That bag is real leather, not plastic.

Real is an adjective that describes *leather*.

> The bag is really fine leather.

Really is an adverb that describes the adjective *fine*.

> That bag is very fine leather.

Very is an adverb that describes and emphasizes *fine*.

bad/badly

Bad is an adjective that describes nouns and pronouns. *Badly* is an adverb that describes verbs, adverbs, and adjectives.

> I ate a bad piece of fish and immediately became ill.

Bad is an adjective that describes *piece*.

> The last time I played basketball, I injured my knee badly.

Badly is an adverb that describes the verb *injured*.

 ## Practice 4.7

Choose the correct word to finish each sentence.

1. This pasta recipe is a (really/real) spicy one.

2. The diamond is (really/real).

3. I did so (badly/bad) on that test!

4. That may have happened because I ate a (bad/badly) breakfast burrito.

5. I bowled with my friends and hurt my back (bad/badly).

6. The clock is running (real/really) fast.

7. Her coach said, "Your running time was (real/very) slow."

8. I had very little sleep last night; I need a cup of coffee (real/really) (bad/badly).

9. I'm staying home because I don't feel (good/well).

10. I need one (good/well) night's sleep.

 Good news! Under ordinary circumstances, adverbs are extremely flexible about where they are placed in a sentence. As you can see, one adverb, *quietly*, can be used correctly in three different places:

1. *Quietly*, the intruder moved around the house.

2. The intruder moved *quietly* around the house.

3. The intruder moved around the house *quietly*.

 ## Prepositions and Prepositional Phrases Act as Adjectives and Adverbs

Prepositions and prepositional phrases link words and phrases to each other. In effect, they act as adjectives and adverbs, as you will see. Here is a partial list of common prepositions:

Common Prepositions

about	above	after	against	along	among
around	at	before	beside	between	for
from	in	into	like	near	of
on	over	under	up	with	

Prepositions give you another way to add description to your sentences. Look at the preposition in the following example:

All the furniture was placed against the walls.

The preposition *against* introduces the phrase *against the walls*. What does the prepositional phrase add to the sentence? It adds a description; it tells where the furniture was placed.

Here's another example:

The new series on Netflix™ has a huge following.

What does *on* Netflix™ describe? It describes series and tells you which series is being talked about—the one on Netflix™.

Finally, look at this sentence:

The students in the auditorium were excited about the final program.

What does *in the auditorium* tell you more about? This phrase tells you about the students and where they are: They are the ones in the auditorium.

Practice 4.8

Choose a preposition from the earlier list to finish each sentence. More than one preposition may apply. Use a preposition only once.

1. One pane _____ glass was broken.

2. My father is teaching _____ the driving school.

3. Have you ever gotten into your car and not realized that your package was _____ top?

4. The library is so close; it's _____ the corner.

5. This problem is _____ you and me.

6. I always keep at least one book _____ the bed.

7. Marie stored too many dishes high _____ the counter.

8. I knew she would never be able to get _____ that cabinet.

9. Perfectly good space stood empty _____ the counter.

10. I'll have a talk _____ her.

Misplaced Prepositional Phrases

Prepositional phrases need to be placed next to the word(s) they describe. What happens if they are not? You will find some very funny results from misplaced prepositional phrases. For example:

The man ran down the stairs in the yellow boots.

According to this sentence, the stairs are in the yellow boots. A simple change of position in the sentence restores order.

The man in the yellow boots ran down the stairs.

Practice 4.9

Find the misplaced prepositional phrases in these sentences. Rearrange each sentence to place these descriptive phrases correctly.

1. The artist on the wall hung his most recent paintings.

   _____

2. The plumber slept after hours of work on the porch hammock.

   _____

3. The doctor in her filing cabinet found her glasses.

   _____

4. My old car has traveled 150,000 miles in the driveway.

   _____

5. The calico cat belongs to me with the brown and gold patches.

   _____

6. The cat belongs to that child with the white tail.

   _____

7. The senator made a negative comment at a congressional meeting about her colleague's family.

   _____

8. The little girl in her toy box found the puzzle.

   _____

9. Laura made chocolate chip cookies for her children with extra nuts.

   _____

10. May placed the lamp next to the plants that she turned on.

   _____

Errors in the use of adverbs occur when speakers and writers fail to think about what the descriptive word describes.

Practice 4.10

Look for an adverb error in each sentence. Give the correction for each incorrect adverb.

1. The swimmer's family cheered loud as she finished first in the meet.

   _____

2. Studying spelling regular will help you remember correct spellings.

   _____

3. This package is real heavy. _____

4. Jake lifted the heavy weight easy. _____

5. We ran frantic from the room. _____

If you had problems with this exercise, you can "dissect" any of the sentences—just the way the examples in this book do—to find the correct answer. For example:

pronoun   verb   object   adj/adv?

I hear you good.

You learned earlier that adverbs describe verbs. You also learned that *good* is an adjective and its adverb form is *well*. The sentence expresses how the subject can hear. *Hear* is a verb. Which word describes the verb *hear*—the adjective *good* or the adverb *well*? You need an adverb, so the answer is *well*.

 ## Practice 4.11

Use everything you've learned in this chapter to correct the error in each sentence. Identify each error and provide the correct word for it.

1. Everyone tells me I talk too loud. _____

2. My family gets along really good. _____

3. Manny said, "I don't feel so good." _____

4. If you want to miss the worst of the traffic, you should leave quick.

   _____

5. Your news was real exciting. _____

6. Marla thought she had done a well job on the assignment. _____

7. I want that promotion so bad! _____

8. Be careful! That knife is particularly sharp. _____

9. My new software works good for this project. _____

10. When I lived at home, my mother always said I played my music too loud.

    _____

5

Verbs Tell Time Perfectly

You know that verbs express time, also called *tense*. They express present, past, and future time: *live*, *lived*, and *will live*. However, your writing and speech often require more than these three tenses in order to clarify time for your reader or listener. You can express even more subtle differences in time by adding one or two helping words such as *has* or *have*. Read on to see the transformation of time.

The Use of Tenses

Do you think you would ever speak or write using just one verb tense? Probably not since not everything occurs in just the present, past, or future time. You agree that you need to switch from past to present to future time according to the context or meaning of your sentences.

When an Action Begins in the Past and Continues into the Present

You know that verbs express time in the present, past, and future.

                  present tense
                    |

PRESENT TENSE: I run a five-mile race each year.

              past tense
               |

PAST TENSE: I ran a five-mile race last year.

              future tense
               |

FUTURE: I will run a five-mile race next year.

Sometimes you want to show that an action began in the past and continues into the present. Inserting the helping word *have* or *has* does that job. The choice between *have* and *has* depends upon the subject of the sentence. If the subject is singular, use *has*. If it is plural, choose *have* (except for first person *I*).

The verbs *have*, *has*, and *had* can be helping verbs or action verbs. They function as action verbs when they are followed by nouns. For example, "I have a pen" tells the action of owning a pen. In a sentence such as "I have acted in many high school plays," *have* plays a different part. Here it is a helping or auxiliary verb; it helps the verb *acted*.

Follow this sequence to understand how to use *have* and *had* to change verb tenses:

> Carla ran a five-mile race for charity.

The running took place in the past. Next, suppose the running took place in the past but continues into the present time. This requires the helping word (also known as auxiliary) *has*.

> Carla has run a five-mile race each year for charity.

Try these rules on some more examples:

> I have run a five-mile race each year since 2019.

The singular subject *I* tells you to use the helping word *have*.

> Jackson has run a five-mile race each year since 2019.

Again we have a singular subject, *Jackson*.

> Naomi and I have run a five-mile race each year since 2019.

For the plural subject *Naomi and I*, use *have* instead of *has*.

When One Past Action Happens Before Another Past Action

The plot thickens: What if one past action happened before another past action? You can make it absolutely clear that the action started in the past before another action. To do this, use *had* in place of *has* or *have*.

> Carla had run a five-mile race for charity before she signed up for the marathon this year.

Notice that the word *had* expresses past time.

Here are more examples of one action happening before another in the past:

> Lizzie had worked here for five years before she moved here.

Both actions occurred in the past (*worked, moved*), but one happened even earlier than the other. Lizzie had worked before she moved. The helping word *had* indicates which action—worked—occurred further in the past.

> Emilio had joined the Marines many years before he transferred to Virginia.

Which past action came first—*joining* or *transferring*? The helping word *had* indicates the earlier past action.

When One Future Action Happens Before Another Future Action

Here's an even more intriguing thought. What if one future action happens before another future action? How is that expressed? You need to add the auxiliary words *will have.*

> I will have read 20 books on the subject before I leave this summer.

The words *will have* show that the reading will be completed before the leaving. The words *will have* indicate an action that will be completed in the future before another future action.

When Actions Are Simultaneous

One more time zone completes the topic. Get ready for simultaneous actions. That simply means two or more actions occurred at the same time. To express this, their tenses must be the same. Here is an example:

> The curtain rose, and the audience applauded.

Rose and *applauded* are both past-tense verbs for actions that occurred simultaneously. You can actually envision the curtain rising at the same time the audience was applauding.

Practice 5.1

Choose the verb form that expresses the correct time.

1. Before she became ill, Della (promised/had promised) to help me.

2. Those two great graphic designers, Maggie and Zoe, (had/has) finished their assignment before the rest of the class finished.

3. I (have/had) raised pigs for several years, and then I decided to raise chickens.

4. They (have/had) saved their money before they looked for a new car.

5. Gabriella (commuted/had commuted) to work for five years before she started to work from home.

Expressing Time with Linking Verbs

Linking verbs express time (tense) and follow the same rules. Just like action verbs, they join with *has*, *had*, and *have* to clarify time even further.

> Margaret grows taller each day.

In this example, the linking verb is *grows*. (*Grows* can be a inking verb or an action verb, depending on the context of the sentence.) The table shows basic ways to express time with this verb.

PRESENT TENSE	PAST TENSE	FUTURE TENSE	WITH HAS, HAD, OR HAVE
I grow	I grew	I will grow	I have/had grown
You grow	You grew	You will grow	You have/had grown
He/she/it grows	He/she/it grew	He/she/it will grow	He has/had grown
We grow	We grew	We will grow	We have/had grown
They grow	They grew	They will grow	They have/had grown

Participles—What Now?

A simple but necessary addition to your understanding of verbs is the use of participles. You know and understand present, past, and future time. You can be more specific about time by correctly using participles. Participles are simply verb forms that come in two varieties: past and present. The present participle uses an *-ing* ending and the past participle is formed by adding *-ed* to the verb.

Past and present participles are two of the five forms or *principal parts* that every verb has. The two tables of verbs give examples of all five forms for several common verbs.

Principal Parts: Action Verbs

PRESENT	PAST	FUTURE	PRESENT PARTICIPLE (WITH AM, HAVE BEEN)	PAST PARTICIPLE (WITH HAS, HAD, OR HAVE)
help	helped	will help	helping	helped
smile	smiled	will smile	smiling	smiled
play	played	will play	playing	played

Here are some examples of how participles are used in action verbs:

PRESENT:	I *help* my son with homework every night.
PAST:	I *helped* my friend get a job.
FUTURE:	I *will help* you, too.
PRESENT PARTICIPLE:	I *am helping* most of my friends, too.
PAST PARTICIPLE:	I *had helped* your friend Barry before I met you.

Principal Parts: Linking Verbs and Participles

PRESENT	*PAST*	*FUTURE*	*PRESENT PARTICIPLE (WITH AM)*	*PAST PARTICIPLE (WITH HAS, HAD, OR HAVE)*
grow	grew	will grow	growing	grown
become	became	will become	becoming	become
appear	appeared	will appear	appearing	appeared

Here are some examples of how linking verbs are used with participles:

PRESENT:	I *feel* tired because I didn't sleep well last night.
PAST:	I *felt* tired yesterday as well.
FUTURE:	I *will feel* tired as long as I don't sleep.
PRESENT PARTICIPLE:	I *am feeling* more tired this afternoon.
PAST PARTICIPLE:	At our last visit, I *had felt* more ready to work.

Tenses of *to Be*

The verb *to be* (including *is*, *are*, *was*, etc.) requires a chart of its own. *Be* has many different forms, depending upon tense and number (*am*, *is*, *are*, *was*, *were*). However, those forms account only for the past and present tenses. The future tense uses the word *will* plus *be*. Finally, *be* combines with the helping words *to*, *will*, *can*, *could*, *would*, and *should*.

The following lists show the correct use of these words in the singular as well as the plural forms.

Present Time, Singular and Plural

(I) I *am* an aspiring astronaut.

(You) You *are* my copilot.

(He) Manuel *is* an experienced driller.

(She) Jodi *is* an operating room nurse.

(It) Your dog *is* a Jack Russell terrier.

Who *is* the newest student in our class?

(We) Seth and I *are* chairmen of that committee.

(You, plural) You and your boss *are* always so pleasant to each other.

Who *are* the candidates?

(They) Betsy and Ana *are* roommates.

Past Time, Singular and Plural

(I) I *was* a very small baby.

(You) You *were* much larger than I was.

(He) Rubio *was* very entertaining.

(She) Samantha *was* my best friend in ninth grade.

(It) The decoration *was* fancier than I had ever seen.

Who *was* the guest speaker?

(We) Nillie and I *were* the planners.

(You, plural) You two *were* successful.

Who *were* your helpers?

(They) Tim and Rico *were* the first to offer help.

Future Time, Singular and Plural

(I) I *will be* a senior next year.

(You) You *will be* the best soccer player in the league.

(He) Manuel *will be* an experienced driller.

(She) Jodi *will be* an operating room nurse.

(It) Your dog *will be* a Jack Russell terrier.

Who *will be* the newest student in our class?

(We) Seth and I *will be* chairmen of that committee.

(You, plural) You *will be* pleasant to each other.

Who *will be* the candidates?

(They) Betsy and Ana *will be* roommates.

Finally, can you add these words to the following sentences? Choose one phrase to fill each space.

to be   can be   would be   should be

1. I _____ there on time.

2. You _____ proud of your accomplishment.

3. I plan _____ at the meeting.

4. It _____ a good idea to make a plan.

Did you use the phrases in the following order? There are a few different possibilities.

1. can be/should be

2. should be/can be

3. to be

4. would be

Using Verbs in the Past, Present, and Future

You've worked with sentences in the present, past, and future time. As you probably realized, though, time may not be that simple. For example, you may want to express two past actions but show that one occurred before the other. How do you accomplish that? Read on for answers.

Using Helping Words to Convey Time

It is usually a simple matter to show an action that started in the past and continues into the present. To review, look at the following example:

Franco has visited his parents in Italy every year since 2019.

Franco started visiting his parents in Italy in 2019, and he's still doing that every year. Adding the helping word *has* makes the timing clear.

As you will see in the following sentence, writers and speakers get into trouble when they sprinkle the words *has* and *have* too freely over the sentence.

INCORRECT: Henry has commuted to Detroit for two years, and he has been tired of commuting.

CORRECT: Henry has commuted to Detroit for two years, and he is tired of
commuting.

Henry's commuting to Detroit started in the past and continues into the present. Now Henry is tired of commuting. The word *has* indicates the earlier past action.

Practice 5.2

Reword the following sentences by either inserting or deleting the helping words has *or* have *where necessary. Caution: Be ready for spelling changes of the verbs.*

1. Sydney rides her bike every day since she got it for her birthday last year.

   _____

2. Mica has wore that coat on cold days since she had bought it five years ago.

   _____

3. Mr. Astrella taught for 10 years and is teaching at the same school today.

   _____

4. Enrico raised flowers for many years and raises them in his greenhouse today.

   _____

5. John and Erin raised two children, and now they have spent time traveling.

   _____

6. Eric stood last in line since he arrived later.

   _____

7. Wendy and Ana have babysat for us since we had moved here.

   _____

8. Mia camped in our backyard since we moved here three summers ago.

   _____

9. You and she commuted together for five years before she changed jobs.

   _____

10. Before the election, both candidates promised prosperity for all.

    _____

Using Helping Words with Two Past Actions

At times, you may want to express two past actions and show that one occurred before the other. The earlier past action requires a helping word.

Elias had interviewed for the position three times before he got the job.

Which past action came first—interviewing or getting the job? The helping word *had* indicates the earlier past action—interviewing.

> Too much of a good thing—that is, too many helping words—makes a sentence wrong.
>
> INCORRECT: Before the mechanic had replaced the battery, our car had needed a repair every six weeks or so.

What happened further back in the past—the car needing repair or our mechanic replacing the battery? In the past, our car had needed repair every six weeks or so. What happened next? The mechanic replaced the battery. Which is the only action that requires a helping word? The answer is *needed*, because it happened first in the past.

CORRECT: Before the mechanic replaced the battery, our car had needed a repair every six weeks or so.

Practice 5.3

Insert or delete the helping word had *where necessary.*

1. Leon had washed the car before Priya had arrived.

   _____

2. Women had voted for more than 75 years before the issue of women's rights had taken hold.

   _____

3. Ceil and Dick has moved before they have sold their house.

   _____

4. Someone told me that you had studied English before you had moved to the United States.

   _____

5. I had had no cash because I had lost my wallet.

   _____

6. Susie had driven the rental car 100 miles before she had realized she was late.

   _____

7. I had suffered the pain of a separated shoulder for a week before I had called a doctor.

_____

8. After we had bought the bedroom set, we had seen the deep scratches on the headboard.

_____

9. Paulie had resisted working out before he had met Jeannie.

_____

10. Ceil had babysat for us before she had entered middle school.

_____

Using Helping Words to Convey the Completion of a Future Action Before Another One

To show the completion of one future action before another future action, use the words *will have* with the verb. Here are two examples:

> The ship will have spent 21 days at sea before it reaches port.

> By the time I email you, I will have prepared and typed the report.

Which actions happen in the future before other future actions? In the first sentence, *will have spent* happens before *reaches*. In the second sentence, *will have prepared and typed* will happen in the future before *email*.

Be clear about which action will be completed in the future before another future action. Use *will have* with this action word. Do not overuse *will have* with other verbs in the sentence.

INCORRECT: If she's not careful, my daughter will have charged too much to my credit card before I will have closed the account.

CORRECT: If she's not careful, my daughter will have charged too much to my credit card before I close the account.

Using Helping Words with Simultaneous Actions

Simultaneous actions are easy to construct. Two actions must simply occur at the same time.

CORRECT: The cost of loans went down, and we immediately bought a new car.

Errors occur when writers insert unnecessary helping words in the sentence.

INCORRECT: As we raised our tent for camping, huge black clouds had
                appeared above us.

Since the two actions—*raised* and *appeared*—occurred simultaneously, there's
no need to insert a helping verb with either verb.

CORRECT: As we raised our tent for camping, huge black clouds appeared
                above us.

 ## Practice 5.4

Insert or delete helping words to make each sentence correct.

1. As soon as I said his name, I had known I was wrong.

   _____

2. Steve will have overspent his travel allowance before his boss will have
   checked the account.

   _____

3. Just before the class walked out of the room, Mr. Rumpler noticed the book
   on the floor.

   _____

4. The car sounded strange for several hours before it stopped running.

   _____

5. Leslie will have improved her English by the time she will have finished
   this book.

   _____

6. Julie had added an extra cup of flour before she had realized it.

   _____

7. I walked out into the rain and had opened my umbrella.

   _____

8. By the time Amanda will have gotten home, Essie will have cleaned the
   entire house.

   _____

9. As I had walked through the doors, the ticket taker had scanned my ticket.

_____

10. The baby had cried for several hours before it had developed a rash.

_____

Using Linking Verbs to Express Time

Linking verbs express time and follow the same rules. They join with *has*, *had*, and *have* to clarify time.

Linking Verbs

am	is	are	was	were
be (all forms)	look	become	taste	seem
appear	feel	smell	grow	sound

EXAMPLE	*TIME EXPRESSED*
He *is* a judge.	Present
He *was* a negotiator.	Past
He *has been* a judge for six years.	Started in the past and continuing into the present
He *will have been* a judge for 10 years when he retires.	Completion of one future happening before another future happening
Bill and Anita *had been* partners for five years before Bill left town.	Two past linking verbs, with one occurring before the other (The first linking verb requires a helping word.)

Speakers of English use the many forms of *to be* automatically—and usually, but not always, correctly. The table shows the simplest forms of *to be*. Here are some examples of the correct use of this linking verb:

Starting next year, Rubin *will be* working with us full-time.

Your negative answers *are* unacceptable.

They *have been* so helpful this summer.

The days *were* extremely hot.

Forms of *To Be*

Singular

PRESENT	PAST	FUTURE	PRESENT PARTICIPLE	PAST PARTICIPLE
am	was	will be	am being	have been

Plural

PRESENT	PAST	FUTURE	PRESENT PARTICIPLE	PAST PARTICIPLE
are	were	will be	are being	have been

Practice 5.5

In these sentences, insert helping words that help linking verbs clarify time.

1. Monique _____ been in training for the past year.

2. Ellie and Elena _____ been our babysitters since we moved here.

3. Our calico cat _____ become our best friend way before we rescued the pup.

4. Candy the cat _____ been with us 10 years next summer.

5. Jules _____ been a math teacher at the same school for many years.

Practice 5.6

Use all that you have learned in this chapter to correct each sentence.

1. You run a five-mile race each year since 2020.

   _____

2. Ted, Mario, and Alicia run a five-mile race each year since 2020.

   _____

3. All my friends has exercised for many years.

   _____

4. My cousin Vinnie travels across the country and has wrote a book about his adventures.

   _____

5. My neighbors Aisha and Darius and the dog have moved to California, and they have tired of moving.

   _____

6. Fortunately, you had perfected your organizational skills before you had taken that job.

_____

7. I will have spent 60 nights in school before I will have gotten that diploma.

_____

8. If I'm not cautious, our roof will have deteriorated badly before I will have had it repaired.

_____

9. As we pulled into the outdoor theater, the heavy rain had started.

_____

10. Sammy will have been a traffic policeman for 25 years before he will have retired.

_____

6

Pronouns

As you may know already, pronouns are used in place of nouns. There are many pronouns, and they are used under a number of different circumstances. The challenge is to pick the correct pronoun for the particular situation. The correct choice is not always clear to people, but this chapter will help you solve many pronoun mysteries.

Common Pronouns

You already know how to use the most common pronouns—for example, the personal pronouns *I, you, he, she, it, we, they,* and *who.* However, there are another eight categories of pronouns as well. Don't despair! You can get familiar with them.

Don't be surprised if you don't recognize the names of all the pronouns. The wonderful thing about the English language is that you can speak and write correctly without knowing every grammatical term. Still, knowing a few definitely helps.

Pronouns Are Everywhere!

When you need a pronoun, you have eight categories to choose from:

Personal	Reciprocal
Possessive	Relative
Demonstrative	Interrogative
Intensive	Indefinite

Why Use Pronouns?

> Mother said, "Jane, I brought you your dinner in bed only because you are sick. Don't you get used to it."

If you think about the preceding sentence, you realize that writers use pronouns to avoid boring their readers. Remove every pronoun and replace each with a noun. Here's the result:

> Mother said, "Jane, Mother brought Jane Jane's dinner in bed because Jane is sick. Jane, don't get used to dinner in bed."

You can see that this sentence is repetitious.

Another important fact about pronoun use is that, many times, the pronoun refers to a noun that came earlier in the sentence. In the example at the beginning of this section, what does the first *you* refer to?

> "Jane, I brought you your dinner in bed only because you are sick. Don't you get used to it."

You refers to Jane. *Jane* is the *antecedent*, a word that comes before and refers to the pronoun. Antecedent is a grammatical term you should know, because pronouns need something or someone to refer to.

Here is another example:

> My mother was strict. She never allowed me to use her car unless my homework was done.

The word *she* is a clear stand-in for *mother*. The antecedent of *she* is *mother*. The importance of pronouns and their antecedents is clear.

Pronoun Usage

You've learned that words have jobs or functions in sentences. For example, nouns are used as subjects and objects. Personal pronouns take the place of nouns; they are used as subjects and objects. Later you will see that pronouns are very flexible. Under certain circumstances, pronouns can even function as adjectives and nouns.

Read and remember the chart on pronoun usage, and you will never choose the wrong subject or object or possessive pronoun. Subject pronouns are in the first column, and object pronouns that receive the action are in the second column. The third column lists possessive pronouns. Notice that none of the possessive pronouns are spelled with an apostrophe.

Pronoun Usage

SUBJECT PRONOUNS	OBJECT PRONOUNS	POSSESSIVE PRONOUNS
I	me	my, mine
you	you	your, yours
he	him	his
she	her	her, hers
it	it	its
we	us	our, ours
they	them	their, theirs
who	whom	whose

Here are a few examples of pronouns used correctly:

I [subject pronoun] swim very well.

Jim received *it* [object pronoun] yesterday.

She and *I* [pronouns that form the plural subject] are in the same study group in science class.

We gave our study notes to *them* [object of the preposition *to*].

Whom [object of *trust*] do you trust for that position?

If you turn the question around, you can see that *whom* is the object in the sentence "You do trust *whom*?"

Whose [possessive pronoun] phone is that?

The possessive pronoun *whose* acts as an adjective to describe the noun *phone*.

You can see that possessive pronouns show ownership. An interesting characteristic is that they are used either alone—for example, as the subject—or as a descriptive word.

USED ALONE: mine, yours, his, hers, ours, theirs, whose
DESCRIBING A NOUN: my, your, his, her, our, their, whose

In "Hers is the first desk," *hers* is the subject. In "Please find her desk," *her* describes the desk.

Types of Pronouns

Beside personal pronouns, there are other kinds of pronouns as well. You probably use them with little difficulty. You'll find the common errors highlighted as you read this section.

Demonstrative Pronouns

Four pronouns are *demonstrative*, meaning they point out a noun or nouns. The demonstrative pronouns are *this*, *that*, *these*, and *those*.

> Do you like these sale items?

The demonstrative pronoun *these* points out the noun *items*. You can also see that the pronoun *these* functions as an adjective to describe another word.

> These jeans are my favorite ones.

These functions as an adjective telling which jeans.

> That is the one I left somewhere.

That functions as the subject, the way a noun would.

> This is your house.

This functions as the subject of the sentence.

> Those roads are slippery.

Those functions as an adjective to describe *roads*.

Reflexive Pronouns

There are eight reflexive pronouns:

> SINGULAR: myself, yourself, himself, herself, itself
> PLURAL: ourselves, yourselves, themselves

Whether or not you hear or read the following words, they do not exist in Standard English! Remove these from your vocabulary: *hisself, theirselves, themself.*

> INCORRECT: He told hisself that poor grammar was acceptable.

A reflexive pronoun immediately follows the noun or pronoun it emphasizes:

> I myself like the more expensive ones.

> You yourself told me the rules.

She herself will close the bank.

We ourselves will be responsible.

In the first sentence, *myself* is a reflexive pronoun that emphasizes the subject, *I*. In the second, *yourself* emphasizes *you*. In the third, *herself* emphasizes *she*. And in the last sentence, the pronoun *ourselves* emphasizes the subject *we*.

Reciprocal Pronouns

Sentences with plural nouns can use reciprocal pronouns. This kind of pronoun refers to the individual parts of the preceding plural noun. There are always two people or things involved, because *reciprocation* means sharing equally. Reciprocal pronouns include the following:

each other

one another

As you can see, we call these reciprocal pronouns, but they are actually phrases—more than one word.

Find the reciprocal pronouns in the following examples:

The sisters found each other at the ticket booth.

The older sister found the younger sister, and the younger sister found the older one. Therefore, *each other* refers to more than one sister.

The lost child and the dog warmed one another through the night.

The reciprocal pronoun *one another* refers to the child and the dog.

The club members pointed fingers at one another in order to assign blame.

In this sentence, *one another* refers to the club members.

Relative Pronouns

Relative pronouns include *who* and *whose* (subject), *whom* (object), *whose* (possessive), *which* (non-restrictive), *that,* and *which* (restrictive). Relative pronouns relate an adjective clause or a noun clause to the rest of the sentence. We use a relative pronoun to tell us which person or thing we are talking about.

the man *who* identified the star (Which man are we talking about? We're talking about the man who identified the star.)

the car *that* Joe restored (Which car are we talking about? We're talking about the one that Joe restored.)

Who identified the star and *that Joe restored* are both *clauses*.

! Don't Panic!

A clause is simply a group of words that has a subject and a verb but is not a sentence. The entire clause refers to or relates to another word in the sentence. Look for a clause in the following sentence:

The major American novels that she recently finished reading completed the course.

The clause *that she recently finished* has a subject (*she*) and a verb (*finished*), but it is not a sentence. It is a clause that relates to *novels*.

A *non-restrictive clause* is one that can be left out of a sentence without changing its meaning. The following sentence contains a non-restrictive clause:

The science project, which took six months to complete, studied the effect of music on plant growth.

The main idea of the sentence is that the science project studied the effect of music on plant growth. Removing the clause about how long it took to complete does not change the meaning of the main idea.

Restrictive clauses are ones that cannot be removed without changing the meaning of the sentence. These sample sentences contain restrictive clauses:

The box that held the candy was the most sought-after gift.

The chemistry course that he recently completed was the last of his required courses.

What does *that he recently completed* relate to? The answer is *the chemistry course.*

Interrogative Pronouns

The verb *interrogate* means to ask questions. Interrogative pronouns are used to introduce questions. They act as adjectives to describe nouns, as in *whose computer, which desk*. Interrogative pronouns also include *who* and *whom*, subject and object pronouns.

Find the interrogative pronouns in the following sentences.

Whose car shall we take?

Which restaurant are we going to?

Who is your teacher?

You have given your books to whom?

In the first two questions, *whose* describes *car*, and *which* describes *restaurant*. In the third question, the subject is *who*. In the fourth, *whom* is the object of the preposition *to*.

Indefinite Pronouns

Indefinite pronouns refer to a specific but unnamed noun or pronoun. The indefinite pronouns can be singular or plural. They are listed here.

SINGULAR INDEFINITE PRONOUNS	PLURAL INDEFINITE PRONOUNS
another	both
anybody	few
anyone	many
anything	several
each	
either	
everybody	
everyone	
everything	
neither	
nobody	
no one	
nothing	
one	
somebody	
something	
someone	

The person is not specifically named in any of these sentences.

Anybody can come with us.

Anybody can do this work.

Somebody left the lights on.

Pronoun Agreement

Pronouns generally agree in number and gender (male or female) with the nouns they replace. Let's return to the example from early in this chapter:

Mother said, "I brought you your dinner in bed only because you are sick. Don't you get used to it."

In Mother's first sentence, *I* is a pronoun that stands in for *Mother*. Both are singular, and *I* can be either male or female (it is female in this case). Those facts tell us that the pronoun *I* meets the number and gender requirements. The pronoun agrees with the noun it replaces. In the spirit of respect for inclusivity and diversity, many academic and popular publications utilize the traditionally plural pronouns *they* and *their* as a singular pronouns. This choice avoids the use of gendered pronouns and allows the writer or speaker to respond respectfully to the preferred pronoun of a single person whose gender identity is unknown, nonbinary, or gender-nonconforming.

Suggestions:

They and their as singular pronouns.

or

When are *they* and *their* singular?

Functions of Pronouns

Earlier in the book, you learned that various kinds of words, such as nouns and verbs, have certain functions in a sentence. Like nouns, pronouns can serve different functions. Look at the following pair of sentences:

The sun was gone when Jenna went to the pool. She said she was "cloud bathing."

In the second sentence, how does *she* function? The first *she* functions as the subject of the verb *said*. The second *she* is the subject of the linking verb *was*.
Consider another example:

We delivered the pizza to her.

How do the pronouns *we* and *her* function in the preceding sentence? *We* is the subject, and *her* is an object pronoun. We use object pronouns after prepositions—words such as *to, for, about, after,* and so forth. Look for a list of prepositions in Chapter 4.

Using Pronouns Correctly

Pronouns are small words that give some people big problems. Once again, to avoid the problems, think about how pronouns function. When you are in doubt, look at the list below to locate a subject or object pronoun.

Personal Pronouns

These are the personal pronouns you read about at the beginning of the chapter:

Subject Pronouns

I

you

he

she

it

we

they

who

Object Pronouns (Receive the Action)

me

you

him

her

it

us

them

whom

Here are examples of pronouns that substitute for subjects and objects. The first shows how a subject pronoun can replace the original subject:

subject/noun
|
Manuel arrived early on his first day of work.

subject/pronoun
|
He arrived early on his first day of work.

In the following examples, nouns are also used as objects to receive the action of the verb. You can substitute a pronoun for the object as well.

object
|
Jenna gave a green backpack to John.

The object receives the action of the verb. Jenna gave what? She gave the object—green backpack.

object
|
Jenna gave it to him.

The pronoun *it* stands in for *backpack*.

Look at this common mistake that people make when they use personal pronouns. People frequently substitute subject pronouns for object pronouns:

> INCORRECT: I gave a piece of the delicious pie to Jules and he.

You can easily avoid this error. Just use the clues given. You can think about this in two ways.

The first way is to ask yourself whether the pronoun *he* is the subject or an object in the sentence. It is, in fact, an object of the preposition *to*. Now go back to the lists of subject and object pronouns. In which list do you find *he*? It's in the subject list, but this sentence demands an object pronoun. What is the object form of *he*? It is the pronoun *him*.

> CORRECT: I gave a piece of the delicious pie to Jules and him.

Here's a second, even easier, way to choose the right pronoun: When both a noun and a pronoun follow a preposition (*to Jules and him*), delete the noun (*Jules*). Then ask yourself if you would ever say, "I gave a piece of pie to he." You wouldn't, so don't choose that pronoun when the sentence is about more than the one person the pronoun refers to. Because "I gave a piece of the delicious pie to him" is correct, you know that "I gave a piece of the delicious pie to Jules and him" also is correct.

Practice 6.1

Use the clues described in this section to choose the correct pronoun in each sentence.

1. I sent a gift to Juan and (she/her).

2. (Me and Rohan/Rohan and I) carpool to work.

3. Did you call Betsy and (him/he)?

4. Les and (her/she) tried to call me.

5. The last people to board the plane were Aidan and (him/he).

6. Uma tripped over (her/she).

7. The ball almost hit Jones and (he/him).

8. (Me and Scott/Scott and I) traveled to the hockey game together.

9. Have you told Carl and (he/him) that this office is closing?

10. Willie and (her/she) are my favorite people.

Special recognition goes out to the very common error in sentence 2. How many times have you heard or seen phrases like that subject? Me and my friend, me and the dog, me and Bobby—all contain the same error. The sentences contain an object pronoun (*me*), instead of a subject pronoun (*I*), in the subject of the sentence. If the incorrect grammar is not enough, these grammatical forms are also impolite. Always start with the other person first (my friend, the dog, Bobby), and then add yourself:

My friend and I love to eat out once a week.

The dog and I enjoy a three-mile jog each morning.

Bobby and I have known each other since grade school.

Possessive Pronouns

Possessive pronouns act as adjectives that show ownership. Examples: *my, yours, his.*

My friend found his car.

My and *his* act as adjectives to describe nouns.

SINGULAR	PLURAL
my	our
yours	your
his	their (Refer to the Pronoun Agreement section to clarify the use of *their* as a singular pronoun.)
her	
its	

Mine also is a possessive pronoun, but it stands for two words in the sentence. Can you figure out which words *mine* stands for in the following sentence?

The keys left behind were mine.

If you said *my keys*, you were right.

In addition to *mine*, other possessive pronouns that stand for more than one word are *your, yours his/hers, ours,* and *theirs*. All of these pronouns have to be used carefully. You must be sure that you connect the pronoun to its antecedent.

One of the possessive pronouns, *its*, is such a simple word—or is it? One caution: Always be sure that you've chosen the right word, *its* or *it's*. Just remember that *it's* means *it is*. The apostrophe takes the place of the letter *i*. The meaning of the sentence will guide you.

INCORRECT: *Its* time for the children to go to bed.

CORRECT: *It's* time for the children to go to bed.

The second version is correct because *It's* means *It is* time for the children to go to bed.

 ## Practice 6.2

Find the incorrectly used word. Supply the correct one. A hint is given for solving the first one.

1. My neighbor found there dog. _____

   Hint: Is *there* a possessive pronoun? No, it's not even a pronoun! Replace it with either *his, her,* or *their,* depending on the preferred pronoun of your neighbor.

2. Their car is never parked in it's own space. _____

3. Its time for you to leave. _____

4. Is this there's or his? _____

5. Your my best friend. _____

6. My dog pulls on it's collar. _____

7. You're house is painted a beautiful color. _____

8. It's fence is the same wood as mine. _____

9. The workers packed up there truck and left. _____

10. That purse is my one. _____

Possessive pronouns are rarely a problem in this context:

     He took his game and went home.

However, errors are common in the following contexts:

     INCORRECT: Of course, I never approved of him smoking.

Does the sentence require an object pronoun (*him*)? If the sentence ended with the word *him*, it would be correct.

subject/pronoun   object/pronoun
| |

CORRECT: Of course, I never approved of him.

Him is the object of the preposition *of.* But the sentence does not end with *him*. Instead, the sentence ends with *smoking*. (Note: Smoking is a gerund, the -ing form of a verb used as a noun.) The smoking habit belongs to someone; you need to use a possessive pronoun to show the ownership:

CORRECT: Of course, I never approved of *his* smoking.

Here is another example:

INCORRECT: You know I approve of you eating vegetables.

The *eating* belongs to someone; use a possessive pronoun to indicate ownership.

CORRECT: You know I approve of *your* eating vegetables.

 ## Practice 6.3

Complete the sentences with a possessive pronoun. More than one possessive pronoun may be correct.

1. I never approved of _____ driving.

2. We were so impressed with _____ winning the contest.

3. _____ whining doesn't help.

4. We told our son that we would not stand for _____ spending his entire allowance on video games.

5. I think that _____ nail biting is your worst habit.

6. I'm annoyed by _____ eating popcorn in bed.

7. Jared told us he was tired of _____ complaining.

8. Did you ever say that _____ leaving would be a problem?

9. _____ parking in my spot has finally infuriated me!

10. I don't like _____ calling me at work.

Indefinite Pronouns

Indefinite pronouns may be singular or plural. Singular indefinite pronouns include the following:

SINGULAR INDEFINITE PRONOUNS	PLURAL INDEFINITE PRONOUNS	SINGULAR OR PLURAL INDEFINITE PRONOUNS
another	both	all
anybody	few	any
another	many	none
anyone	others	some
anything	several	such
each	they	
either		
everybody		
everyone		
everything		
neither		
nobody		
no one		
nothing		
one		
somebody		
someone		
something		

Plural indefinite pronouns include the following:

both

few

many

several

Use a singular or plural verb to agree with the pronoun. For example:

There are three "houses" in the high school, and each has its own principal.

The pronoun *each* is singular. Therefore, the verb *has* must be singular, too. Decide which verb is required if you change the sentence in the following way:

There are two "houses" in the high school, and both (have/has) (its/their) own principal(s).

Both is a plural pronoun and requires the plural verb *have*. Notice that *its* must then change to the plural pronoun *their*.

A pronoun agrees in number with the word to which it refers with the exceptions noted in the Pronoun Agreement section. Here are a few examples:

> One of my brothers couldn't find his laptop.

His refers to *one*. Both are singular pronouns.

> All of the children display their awards in this case.

Their refers to *all*. Both are plural. Everything must agree.

Practice 6.4

Choose the correct pronoun or verb in each sentence.

1. In this club, everyone (decide/decides) for himself.

2. Each of the girls completed the task to the best of (her/their) ability.

3. Many of the documents (were/was) signed yesterday.

4. Both melons (is/are) ripe.

5. Any toys you can donate (are/is) appreciated.

6. Several of my friends (forget/forgets) my birthday every year.

7. Somebody in the audience (were coughing/was coughing) during the entire performance.

8. One of them (is telling/are telling) the truth.

9. Neither of the girls ever (finish/finishes) her work.

10. No one in the group (leave/leaves) until 6 p.m.

Interrogative Pronouns

The only problem with interrogative pronouns is figuring out what job you want the word to do, what function it fulfills. Remember that *who* and *whom* refer to people. *What* and *which* refer to things. The chart will help you decide if you need a subject pronoun or an object form.

INTERROGATIVE PRONOUN	FUNCTION	REFERS TO
who	subject	person
whom	object	person
whose	subject	person
what	subject/object	thing
which	subject/object	thing

Do you need a subject pronoun or an object form?

(Who/Whom) is coming to the opening of your store?

(Who/Whom) did you meet?

Who is the subject of the first sentence. For the second, to find the subject, turn the sentence around to make a statement. That trick will also reveal the object.

You did meet *whom*?

Now you can see that *you* is the subject, and *whom* is the object.

Practice 6.5

Choose the correct interrogative pronoun in each sentence.

1. (Who/whom) left the laundry in the dryer?

2. Marilyn is the assistant (who/whom) Chris hired.

3. For (who/whom) is that message?

4. (Who/Whom) along with Mike will work on the campaign?

5. From (who/whom) did you borrow that car?

Practice 6.6

Use everything you've learned in this chapter to correct the pronoun errors in these sentences. Identify the incorrect pronoun and give the correct pronoun.

1. I never approved of him smoking in the car or in the house.

_____

2. We gave prizes to Eden and he. _____

3. Whom is up next? _____

4. Me and Alex turned the mattress over. _____

5. I finally saw my cat chase it's tail. _____

6. After eating alone in the restaurant, the customers could not pay for his or her dinners. _____

7. There are two chicken recipes, and both has a distinctive taste.

_____

8. My grandmother sent birthday cards to my brother and I. _____

9. Give those gifts to Elias and she. _____

10. Me and Allie started a book club. _____

7

Punctuation

Few of us think of punctuation as a very exciting topic. However, we need to use it correctly, because without punctuation, writing falls into chaos. Consider the following recipe:

> Preheat oven to 350 degrees in a food processor bowl combine croutons black pepper chili powder and thyme pulse until the mixture is of a fine texture place this mixture into a large bowl combine the onion carrot garlic and red pepper in the food processor bowl pulse until the mixture is finely chopped but not pureed combine the vegetable mixture ground sirloin and ground chuck with the bread crumb mixture season the meat mixture with the salt add the egg and combine thoroughly but avoid squeezing the meat.

If you added periods and capital letters, the recipe would be so much easier to follow. Now, insert the missing periods and capital letters in the recipe. If you know where commas are needed, add those, too. Then check the Answer Key to see the correct punctuation and find out which punctuation skills you need to pay special attention to.

Types of Punctuation

You need to know how to use key punctuation marks. If you master end marks (periods, question marks, exclamation points), plus commas, and semi-colons, you are well on your way to clearer writing.

End Marks

Periods (.), question marks (?), and exclamation points (!) bring thoughts to a conclusion—each in a different way.

A period simply marks the end of a thought. The next sentence will begin with a capital letter. In Chapter 9, you will learn about the places capitals are used, including, of course, at the beginning of a sentence.

Many people protest genetic engineering of food. Many websites publish information about the possible dangers.

A question mark (?) is used at the end of a sentence to signal a direct question.

What should we be doing to make sure our food is safe?

An exclamation point (!) signals excitement. The speaker may be happy or sad or upset as in the example, or the message may be unexpected.

Stop, thief! Give me back my purse!

The Fab Four

You choose an end mark according to the type of sentence you've written. That requirement makes this the perfect time to learn about the four basic sentence types. In English, there are four sentence types. We use them without much thought, but it's interesting to note that each uses a particular end mark, and it's all very logical.

- *Declarative sentences* make statements and convey information or ideas. Whether you are writing a report for work or school, the report is probably composed of mostly declarative sentences. They end in periods.

    Botany is the study of plants.

    Travelers need to be at the airport two hours before their departure times.

- *Imperative sentences* issue commands or requests. This type of sentence ends in a period but may need an exclamation point if the command is sharp and emotional.

    Pass your papers forward.

    Look out on the right!

    Turn off the lights before you leave.

    Halt!

    These four imperative sentences have the same subject—*you*. The subject, *you*, is not stated, but it is understood. The understood *you* is a special feature of imperative sentences.

- *Exclamatory sentences* express strong emotion. An exclamatory sentence is easy to recognize, because it ends in an exclamation mark.

    I can't believe you won the Powerball!

    I lost my new phone!

    This is the worst day of my life!

- *Interrogative sentences* ask questions. They are very easy to recognize, because they always end in a question mark.

    Are you ready yet?

    Is it going to rain again today?

    You still live at the same address, don't you?

How difficult is it to read a recipe without end marks (periods, question marks, and exclamation points) and with no capital letters to follow? You would agree it requires frequent rereading. Reading is much easier and passages are clearer when you know where each sentence ends, when questions are asked, and whether an expression of emotion is intended (not likely in a recipe).

You can see from the opening example that even in a recipe, simple end marks and commas are essential to keeping ideas or procedures straight. A lack of end marks and commas results in confusion.

What corrections would you make to these sentences?

    our town plans a celebration each year

    are you willing to work on the committee

    it's going to be fun

If you made these changes, you were correct.

    Our . . . year.

    Are . . . committee?

    It's . . . fun! (A period would also be correct at the end of this sentence.)

Commas

Commas are useful marks of punctuation, because they divide sentences into understandable parts. A comma can be used anywhere in a sentence as long as the writer is observing comma rules.

    I was on my way to class, but I became very sick.

Here the comma is used between two independent ideas that are joined by the word *but*.

Semicolons

A semicolon is a strong mark of punctuation, stronger than a comma but not quite as strong as an end mark. A semicolon links two closely related thoughts (independent clauses) with no connecting word.

CORRECT: The rising cost of gas has caused a surge in the demand for electric vehicles; many car manufacturers are rushing hybrid and all-electric vehicles into production.

Using Punctuation Correctly

Most people agree that correct punctuation makes our writing clear and meaningful. Following the standard punctuation rules makes your writing understandable to your reader.

Use the Right End Marks

End marks provide clarity and are relatively easy to use correctly.

Insert a period, question mark, or exclamation point in each of these sentences.

Steve Jobs released the first iPhone™ in 2007

How many of you were fortunate enough to purchase one

I was one of the lucky ones

Here are the sentences with correct punctuation:

Steve Jobs released the first iPhone™ in 2007.

How many of you were fortunate enough to purchase one?

I was one of the lucky ones.

Use Commas Correctly

The comma is the most difficult form of punctuation, simply because it has so many uses. The following sentences need commas. Can you see where commas are required? Instruction will follow!

The Constitution establishes the legislative executive and judicial branches of government.

In the winter mornings are very dark.

Can you honestly promise to lower taxes protect the environment support local schools and end unemployment?

Hannah captain of the team was highest scorer.

Here's where the commas belong:

legislative, executive, and judicial (See rule 1 in the following list.)

In the winter, (See rule 2.)

taxes, . . . environment, . . . schools, and end unemployment. (See rule 1.)

Hannah, captain of the team, (See rule 7.)

Consult the following comma style rules whenever you are in doubt about how to punctuate a sentence. As you can see, commas aren't just "sprinkled" in sentences. Each one should have a reason to be used.

Comma Style Rules

1. To ensure clarity, use commas to separate items in a series. With items in a series, the comma before *and* is called the Oxford comma. Some grammar experts consider this comma optional.

   Ted runs outside in spring, summer, and fall.

2. Use a comma to separate an introductory word or phrase from the rest of the sentence.

   Before last year, I had never traveled out of this country.

3. In an address, separate the city and state with a comma.

   Boise, Idaho

4. Use a comma to separate the day from the year and the year from the rest of the sentence.

   We arrived on May 1, 2021, and stayed for a year.

5. Commas separate more than one descriptive word describing the same word.

   Garden enthusiasts like colorful, fast-growing flowers.

6. A comma follows the salutation in a friendly letter. A comma also follows the closing in a friendly letter as well as in a business letter.

   Dear Benita,
   Sincerely,
   Bernie

7. Commas separate words or groups of words that interrupt the flow of a sentence, including names in direct address.

Today, I must tell you, is the last day to submit a proposal to the council.

No, Mr. Ramirez, the store doesn't open until 10 a.m.

8. Commas separate two complete thoughts that are joined by a connecting word such as *for, or, and*, or *but*.

I will write an updated résumé for the upcoming interview, and I have every hope that I will get the job.

9. Commas separate a direct quotation from the rest of the sentence.

"I'm not ready yet," she said.

James responded, "We're going to be late!"

"I don't care," she said, "and I'm not going to rush."

10. The words *therefore, however, nevertheless*, and *inasmuch as* are set off by commas when they interrupt a complete thought.

Should we, therefore, call nuclear power skeptics totally without merit?

Avoid these common comma errors:

1. When a sentence begins with a complete thought followed by an incomplete thought, a comma is not used.

    INCORRECT: Ted worked out for 45 minutes, before he ate breakfast.
    CORRECT: Ted worked out for 45 minutes before he ate breakfast.

2. If the sentence has one subject and two actions, a comma is not used to separate the two actions.

    INCORRECT: Professor Timmins always begins on time, and ends on time, too.
    CORRECT: Professor Timmins always begins on time and ends on time, too.

 ## Practice 7.1

Identify where commas are needed according to the previous rules.

1. Yes General White please tell us how you feel about that.

2. Please walk the dog take out the garbage and lock the back door before we leave.

3. My son said "I'll only do that after you tell me where we're going."

4. I was about to turn off the lights and leave but you stopped me and asked a question.

5. If I could get a job I would move to Mesa Arizona.

6. Craig worked on developing his new program after normal working hours.

7. I have finished my research paper but I'm not sure if it is long enough.

8. Wednesday I have to confess is the worst day of the week for me.

9. I was leaving the gas station when the attendant yelled "Lady, disconnect the hose!"

10. I especially like to plant colorful fast-growing flowers.

Use Semicolons Properly

Like end marks, the semicolon is a strong mark of punctuation. The semicolon has the power to end a thought in the middle of a sentence! You can connect two related thoughts by using a semicolon. The semicolon adds variety and power to your writing.

> We said we would meet our friends in Tulsa; we never got there.

It may be tempting to use just a comma after *Tulsa*. That would be wrong. Commas alone don't have the power to connect two complete thoughts.

> INCORRECT: We said we would meet our friends in Tulsa, we never got there.

This is now a run-on sentence, also known as a comma fault. To correct this misstep, you can insert a semicolon or use a connecting word (also called a conjunction) and a comma, as in comma rule 8.

Using Commas and Semicolons with Connecting Words

A *conjunction* is a connecting word that either makes two ideas equal or makes one of those ideas unequal or dependent. We call the following conjunctions coordinating because they bring two equal ideas together. Coordinating conjunctions include *for, and, nor, but, or, yet,* and *so.* In the following sentence, two ideas are equal.

> You are the best student president we've had, so we're giving you a commendation.

In the next example, one idea (after the comma) can stand alone, and the other cannot.

> Because the QLED TV is much too expensive, I'm not going to buy it.

The idea that cannot stand alone starts with another kind of conjunction, a *subordinating* conjunction, *because.* That makes sense since *subordinating* means making something less important. In this sentence, the part that cannot stand alone can be deleted without changing the main idea of the sentence: *I'm not going to buy it.*

Subordinating conjunctions also join two clauses. One of those clauses (the independent clause) can stand alone as a complete thought. The other one (the dependent clause) cannot.

dependent clause   independent clause

| |

Although it was raining heavily, we all went camping.

The subordinating conjunction *although* joins two clauses: the dependent clause *although it was raining heavily* and the independent clause *we all went camping.*

Subordinating Conjunctions

after	although	as	because	before	how
if	once	since	than	that	though
till	until	when	where	whether	while

Use a comma at the end of the dependent clause when the dependent clause comes first. If you reverse the sentence, you don't need a comma between the clauses.

> We all went camping although it was raining heavily.

While some sentences that use a connecting word are correct with a comma, others demand a semicolon. To make good punctuation choices, it helps to understand the difference between coordinating and subordinating conjunctions. You've made a start here, but in Chapter 12, you will learn even more about building sentences with commas and semicolons.

In most cases, use a comma before a coordinating conjunction.

> The store is open every day, but the jewelry department is open on weekends only.

You need to avoid confusion, however, if there are commas in either clause. In that case, use a semicolon before the coordinating conjunction.

> The store is open every day; but that department, the jewelry department, is open on weekends only.

Practice 7.2

In each sentence, decide where a semicolon is needed (if at all).

1. No one will forget Brady's bravery in the war he certainly earned the Purple Heart.

2. I will donate more hours to tutoring than I had promised.

3. The contract you wrote is unfair to me I can't sign it.

4. Tory missed another practice she will be sitting on the bench at the next game.

5. My friend just moved here from California she wants me to show her the sights.

6. I left keys, my purse, and my lunch on the bus!

7. Taste my sandwich it is delicious.

8. Have a good trip and enjoy your vacation.

9. I watched "Dancing with the Stars" last night I was so happy that couple number 3 won!

10. I love a gentle rainstorm raindrops on my window put me to sleep so quickly.

Practice 7.3

Correct the following sentences. Insert commas, semicolons, periods, or question marks as needed.

1. I made the dress myself I proudly wore it to the prom

2. Jamie's sure she wants to go, I'm waiting to hear from Matthew.

3. Are you ready for exams.

4. You infuriate me

5. Cari will make the main course for dinner, I'll bring the dessert.

6. Choose from brownies apple pie cupcakes and carrot cake for dessert.

7. I streamed three wonderful movies in one weekend

8. Really Charlie how do you feel about going to summer school

9. You sent the letter to Providence Rhode Island on February 15 2022 didn't you

10. Plumbers fix rusty broken pipes.

Separating Complete Thoughts

You can separate complete thoughts in four ways:

1. Use a period after each complete thought.

   Andre, Jill, and Elias went camping. They decided to hike in the early morning.

2. Use a comma and a connecting word—*so, for, or, and, but, nor*—between complete thoughts.

   Andre couldn't make it to the summit and back before dark, so he decided to camp for the night.

3. To avoid confusion, use a semicolon between two complete thoughts when one of the thoughts contains commas.

   Andre, Jill, and Elias couldn't make it to the summit and back before dark; so they decided to camp for the night.

4. Use a semicolon and a comma when you connect complete thoughts with these words: *therefore, however, nevertheless, inasmuch as*.

   I never received an invitation; therefore, I won't go to the party.

Practice 7.4

In the following sentences, determine where periods, semicolons, and/or commas are needed.

1. I don't like the new schedule I'll wait for next term to sign up.

2. My cousin Geri whom you met last year arrived yesterday and in spite of her 24-hour trip she wants to see the sights today.

3. I waited too long to ice my ankle therefore it became swollen.

4. My youngest cousin Jenna went on her first plane ride to Orlando Florida and of course she loved it.

5. The plasterers planned to start work today however their plan was ruined when only two workers showed up.

6. Put the ingredients on your list or you will surely forget them.

7. We'll take the 10 p.m. train you take the earlier one.

8. Geometry, history, and English are taught in the morning so I've decided to start going to bed much earlier.

9. I love music however I was never very persistent about practicing the piano.

10. Lowercase letters follow semicolons only proper nouns such as names are capitalized after a semicolon.

 # Practice 7.5

Use everything you've learned in this chapter to correct these sentences.

1. Marilyn Joe and Tim were my teammates last year.

   _____

2. Rick do you remember them

   _____

3. Some people talk too much they're usually not too popular.

   _____

4. Stop thief

   _____

5. I expect to graduate on June 16 2024.

   _____

6. Amory president of her class is very well thought of.

   _____

7. Walk run or sprint but get here on time.

_____

8. I've just learned that we're moving to Boston Massachusetts.

_____

9. Ryan will you go with me

_____

10. The warm moist cake was so delicious.

_____

Punctuation, Continued

You learned in Chapter 7 that punctuation is used to clarify writing. That is true, as you will see in this chapter as well.

More Types of Punctuation

This chapter covers quotation marks, colons, apostrophes, dashes and hyphens, and parentheses and brackets. Each mark presents its own challenge, but most follow a logical set of rules. A brief explanation of each mark of punctuation starts the chapter. Then, more in-depth study follows.

Quotation Marks

Of all the remaining punctuation, quotation marks rival the comma in that there are so many different ways to use them. However, there are logical reasons for each of the rules. Without quotation marks, we'd never know who was speaking or to whom. Be calm and be logical. You will succeed. Here are two examples:

> "That's an excellent idea," Roger said.
>
> "That," Roger said, "is an excellent idea."

Colons

While a semicolon joins two sentences, a colon joins a sentence to a group of words that finish the thought with a list, illustration, or explanation. Here are two examples:

> I have a method for getting homework done more efficiently: Make a list of the assignments, gather books and tools, and attack the most difficult part first.

Gather these supplies for your trip: bottled water, fresh fruit, bread sticks, and cheese.

Apostrophes

An apostrophe is used to mark the omission of a letter or to indicate possession. For example, a letter is omitted in *weren't* and *isn't*. The apostrophe indicates possession in *cat's tail* and *officers' caps*.

Ain't is not a word and is never an acceptable substitute for *is not*.

Dashes and Hyphens

Although dashes (short and long, – and —) and hyphens (-) look almost alike, they are used for different purposes. These examples show common uses of dashes:

LONG DASH: My parents told me to call if I was going to be late—even 15 minutes—so they wouldn't worry.

SHORT DASH: The Boston Red Sox beat the Yankees 4–3.

The hyphen joins compound words and two-word adjectives such as *mother-in-law* and *one-way street*.

Parentheses and Brackets

Parentheses enclose words that are not absolutely necessary to the thought of the sentence.

I have a college interview on April 10 (it's either a Thursday or a Friday).

If you want to enclose another phrase that is already inside parentheses, use brackets for clarity.

Our business takes us all over Europe (to Italy [Milan], Germany [Munich], and Switzerland [Zurich]).

Using Punctuation Correctly

Learn and practice these rules. They'll make your writing clearer and will help your reader to follow your thoughts more precisely.

Using Quotation Marks

The first thing you need to know about quotation marks is that they set off the exact words of a speaker. That's really the easy part.

The young boy said, "I quit. I'm taking my ball and going home."

What were the boy's exact words? They appear inside the quotation marks: "I quit. I'm taking my ball and going home."

Why is the following example not a quotation?

> The young boy said that he was quitting. He was taking his ball and going home.

This example does not give the boy's exact words; it is a report describing what the boy said. What one word makes this a report? The word *that* is your clue to it being a report.

The more difficult decision regarding quotation marks usually comes when you need to decide where punctuation goes within the quotes. A period always goes inside the quotes.

INCORRECT: "I quit. I'm taking my ball and going home".
 CORRECT: "I quit. I'm taking my ball and going home."

Other forms of punctuation are also used with quotation marks. For example, a comma is placed between the speaker and the words spoken.

> The department manager said, "Three associates must work overtime on Friday."

If the quotation is in two parts, set off both parts with quotation marks.

> "Stop filling that container," his mother cautioned. "The juice will spill all over the counter."

Do not capitalize the first letter of the second part of the quotation unless it signals the beginning of a new sentence, as it does in the previous quotation.

> "Stop filling the container," his mother cautioned, "or the juice will spill all over the counter."

If a sentence requires a semicolon, place it after the closing quote.

> You said, "Stop filling the container"; therefore, I stopped.

Use only one form of punctuation at the end of a quotation. When the entire sentence is a question but the quoted portion is not, place a question mark after the closing quotation marks. When the quoted portion is a question, place the question mark inside the quotes.

> Did Manuel say, "I'll gladly work the extra hours"?

> Manuel said, "Did you say I could work extra hours?"

In the first example, the entire sentence is a question. In the second example, only the quoted portion is a question.

Remember, use only one form of punctuation at the end of a quotation. When the entire quotation is an exclamation but the quoted portion is not, place an exclamation mark after the closing quotation marks.

I would have screamed if you'd called and said, "I have to cancel again"!

When the quoted portion is an exclamation, place the exclamation mark inside the quotes.

She heard a very loud voice scream, "I've had an accident!"

Use single quotation marks for a quotation within a quotation.

A student asked, "Is it true that Aristotle said, 'A friend to all is a friend to none'?"

Use quotation marks to enclose titles of chapters, articles, poems, or any part of a magazine or book. If the quoted title is followed by a comma, the comma is placed inside the quotation marks.

The fourth chapter of *Unplug Your Kids*, entitled "The Early Elementary Years," is about the role of media in children's lives.

 Practice 8.1

Correct the following sentences by inserting capital letters, quotation marks, and other forms of punctuation wherever they are needed.

1. My daughter said, please let me drive to school today I promise I'll be home by 4 p.m.

2. Please let me drive to school today my daughter said. I promise I'll be home by 4 p.m. she continued.

3. The doctor warned don't take antibiotics for every cold therefore I stopped.

   (Hint: You need a semicolon in this sentence, but where should it be placed?)

4. How could you have been on time she asked. You got up an hour late.

5. Charlotte asked, can you remember if Judy said I'll be in at 1 p.m. today.

6. Once again the teacher reminded the class to upload our reports by Friday, place our names on the first page, and include a Works Cited page.

7. Did you remember to return your books to the library Ms. Blake asked or are you waiting to be reminded again

8. I read three mysteries including *The Blade The London Terror* and *Mysteries of the Deep.*

9. When I said meet me at noon I didn't mean 1 p.m.

10. The job counselor said bring a pen, paper, and recent job listings with you.

Using Colons

You read earlier that a colon joins a sentence to a group of words that finish the sentence with a list, illustration, or explanation. In a sentence that contains a colon, the portion before the colon can always stand on its own. If, for some reason, it cannot stand alone, do not use a colon.

> : a large can of plum tomatoes, lasagna noodles, olive oil, salt, pepper, and shredded cheese.

Notice that the words following the colon cannot stand alone; they do not form a sentence. What's missing?

> To make preparing lasagna easier, always start by assembling the ingredients

This portion of the sentence that can stand alone is missing.

A colon can also introduce an explanation:

> Her summer days follow a pattern: She gets up late, dresses for the beach, and packs her lunch.

Notice that the information after the colon is also a sentence. The word *she* requires a capital letter.

A common colon error involves adding a verb at the end of the sentence before the colon:

> Her summer days follow a pattern, which is: She gets up late, she dresses for the beach, and she packs her lunch.

When the first sentence ends in *which is*, the portion of the sentence before the colon can no longer stand alone. To avoid the error, do not use a verb (in this case, *is*) before a colon.

Other uses of the colon are in business letters and expressions for time of day. In a business letter, use a colon after the salutation.

> Dear Dean Edwards:
>
> Dear Ms. Klein:
>
> Dear Dr. Ambrose:

Use a colon between numbers to show the time in hours and minutes.

> 10:15 a.m.

Practice 8.2

Correct the following for use of colons and capital letters, or indicate "no change" if no change is needed.

1. Dear Mom and Dad: _____

2. I can meet you at the mall at 11: a.m. _____

3. For our trip bring the following a sleeping bag, small cooking utensils, and a tent. _____

4. At the meeting, Sara placed a small pile of papers in front of each person which was: an agenda, a list of expectations for each member, and a list of dates for future meetings. _____

5. Prepare to complete these items each morning turn on the computer, turn up the heat to 68 degrees, make written notes of messages from the answering machine. _____

6. I want a secretary who can do the following answer the phone, take correct messages, and use Microsoft Word and Excel. _____

_____

7. A first-aid kit should include these items Gauze, tape, and aspirin.

_____

8. Her recipe for brownies included eggs, flour, sugar, and butter. _____

_____

9. There are three countries in North America Canada, Mexico, and the United States _____

10. Remember three things Take extra money with you, dress for cold weather, and call me if you need a ride. _____

Using Apostrophes

Insert an apostrophe in a word to show that a letter is missing: *haven't*, *weren't*, and *don't* are examples. In each of these words, the apostrophe helped to create a negative word.

haven't = have not

weren't = were not

don't = do not

As mentioned earlier, the one negative word that should never be used is *ain't*. *Ain't* is used—incorrectly—in place of *am not*. Remove this word from your vocabulary!

Apostrophes are also used with -*s* to show possession.

> one cat's tail, two cats' tails

For the singular *cat*, the possessive form is *cat's*. For the plural *cats*, the possessive form is *cats'*.

Placement of the apostrophe with a plural noun also depends on how a word forms its plural. The following table summarizes the rules for placing the apostrophe to make plural nouns possessive.

SINGULAR	PLURAL	RULE
woman's	women's	When the plural requires an internal spelling change, add -'s.
deer's	deer's	When the singular and plural are spelled the same, the apostrophe goes in the same place.
lady's	ladies'	The plural of *lady* requires a change of spelling from *y* to *ies*. For a plural ending in -*s*, add an apostrophe at the end.

 ! Don't mistake *it's* for a possessive form. It means *it is*. *Its* is possessive: The dog licked *its* paws. Note that *his* and *hers* are the possessive forms of *he* and *she*. Possessive pronouns don't have apostrophes: for example, *yours, theirs, ours*.

Finally, to avoid confusion, use the apostrophe to show the plurals of letters.

> That word has four *s*'s in it.

 # Practice 8.3

Correct the sentences by adding or deleting apostrophes, as necessary.

1. This books cover is badly torn.

2. The bear shook it's huge body.

3. To dot your is and cross your ts is a very old saying.

4. Dont wait for me; my plane doesnt arrive until midnight.

5. The childrens department is on the third floor.

6. My dogs ears stand up straight when hes angry.

7. I read that, in many parts of the world, goats milk is used more often than cows milk.

8. The horses saddle was old and much used.

9. Its Charlie's birthday.

10. We're amazed at how fast our dog gobbles down it's food.

Using Dashes and Hyphens

If you use a keyboard of any sort, you know that a dash may be one of two lengths: short or long. The short dash is called an *en dash* because it is the approximate width of a capital *N*. The en dash is used to connect numbers and sometimes words and replaces the word *to*.

> We lived in New Jersey during the years 2016–2021.

> Before the exam, I had to read Chapters 1–20.

> The New York–Chicago train leaves at noon.

> The Celtics won 78–67.

If you use an *en* dash with the year of someone's birth but give no year of death, you mean that person is still living.

> Dr. Brown (1975–)

This means Dr. Brown was born in 1975 and is still living.

The longer dash is called the *em dash*. As you may have guessed, the em dash is so called because it is the width of a capital *M*. Use an em dash on either side of an interrupting thought:

> Choose a movie—you know what I like—and we'll meet after work.

As you can see, the em dash emphasizes the interrupting thought. One caution: Don't use too many em dashes, or they lose their impact.

If your word processor doesn't have an em dash, simply type two hyphens with no space on either side.

The em dash is unique in that it can be used with two other forms of punctuation, the question mark and the exclamation point.

Your quarterly report—the one you almost forgot about!—was very well done.

 ## Practice 8.4

Indicate where en or em dashes are needed.

1. Our team won one championship during the years 2018–2021.

   _____

2. We plan on taking the Boston New York train at 11:30. _____

   _____

3. I studied for the exam for six months with excellent results. _____

   _____

4. We live on the Massachusetts New Hampshire border. _____

   _____

5. I pay the bills don't call me for money and I'm broke most of the time.

   _____

The hyphen is usually grouped with the dashes because it looks so much like a dash. However, the hyphen has an entire set of rules to itself.

Some people prefer to think of hyphens as a part of spelling because their most common use is to join compound words, such as *mother-in-law* and *weight-bearing exercise*. Here are the rest of the hyphen rules.

Use a hyphen to link two or more words serving as a single adjective before a noun.

   two-way streets

   chocolate-covered cupcakes

However, don't use a hyphen if the compound comes after the noun.

   The cupcakes were chocolate covered.

Use a hyphen with prefixes and suffixes in some situations. Use it with the prefixes *ex-* (former), *all-*, and *self-*. Use a hyphen between a prefix and a capitalized word. Use one with the suffix *-elect*. Use a hyphen to join a prefix or suffix to figures or letters.

> ex-aide
>
> all-included
>
> self-starter
>
> all-American
>
> president-elect
>
> mid-200s

Use a hyphen to avoid confusion regarding the meaning of a word.

> re-sign the contract
>
> semi-independent

In the first example, the hyphen avoids confusion with *resign*, meaning to leave a job. In the second, a hyphen after *semi-* makes the word easier to read.

When a full word doesn't fit at the end of a line, use a hyphen where you break the word. Always break a word between syllables.

> un-finished
>
> mis-spelled

For words ending in *-ing*, break between double consonants. If a word doesn't have double consonants, hyphenate at the suffix.

> run-ning
>
> sun-ning
>
> driv-ing

If the word is already hyphenated, divide at the hyphen.

> mass-produced

Use a hyphen with compound numbers.

> fifty-three
>
> twenty-nine

 # Practice 8.5

Insert hyphens where they are needed. Delete them where they are not needed.

1. I love chocolate covered strawberries. _____

2. My father in law has always been overbearing. _____

3. I'll take twenty two small mushrooms. _____

4. He's seen as an all powerful influence. _____

5. We've used out of date equipment since I started to work here.

   _____

6. She has a low budget job. _____

7. My computer expert fine tuned my old computer. _____

8. We know that people should not have more x rays than are absolutely
   necessary. _____

9. The ice cream was sprinkle-covered. _____

10. Before the vote, did you know who the chairman elect would be?

    _____

Using Parentheses and Brackets

There's an easy way to know if you've used parentheses correctly. When you read the sentence, you should be able to skip the words in parentheses and still have the sentence make sense. If the sentence no longer makes sense, the parentheses are used incorrectly.

> I expect to make two hundred dollars ($200).

The previous sentence is clearly understandable without the part in parentheses. Use parentheses to enclose letters or numbers in a list.

> The chapters include (1) infancy, (2) early childhood, and (3) early school years.

When the parentheses are within a sentence, do not use a capital letter or final punctuation mark (except a question mark) inside parentheses.

> I completed the half-marathon (still standing) in four hours.

However, when the parentheses hold a complete sentence, the punctuation goes inside the parentheses.

> Washington Irving wrote the story. (He was born in 1783.)

Finally, brackets may be used inside parentheses or a quotation. Use brackets to enclose a comment that interrupts a direct quotation.

> Malcom Green was named chairman for 2022 (an honorary [unpaid] position).

> We studied parts of Canada (the Province of Quebec [including Montreal] and the Province of Ontario [including Ottawa]).

Practice 8.6

Insert parentheses and brackets where they are needed.

1. I've never shopped at the local malls Westlake Mall, Macy's, Middleboro Mall, Kohl's.

2. I love vegetables green beans broccoli asparagus, yellow corn and peppers.

3. We hoped to buy shoes made in other countries (Italy Florence, France Paris, England London).

4. Before you leave for school, remember to do this: 1. Eat breakfast, 2. Make your bed, 3. Walk the dog.

5. Sharon finished all her chores in 15 minutes or was it 10?

6. Use a separate bowl for the dry ingredients sugar, flour, salt.

7. Charles grew up in a big house some two dozen rooms, six bathrooms.

8. I've lived in small towns 250 residents! and large ones.

9. The captain said, "Plan on leaving the station within one minute absolutely no longer than two of receiving the call."

10. My first week's pay was three hundred dollars $300.

Practice 8.7

Use everything you've learned in this chapter to correct the punctuation in these sentences.

1. These are the ingredients I need to buy flour, sugar, and eggs.

   _____

2. I promised myself no matter what else happened that I would take a vacation.

   _____

3. The teacher said don't forget the quiz on Friday.

   _____

4. The teacher said, "that there would be a quiz on Friday."

_____

5. I havent seen you in so long.

_____

6. One of the tables legs is loose.

_____

7. My dog licked it's dish clean.

_____

8. Take the New York Miami train.

_____

9. Harrison is the expresident of our club.

_____

10. The all inclusive price is a bargain.

_____

9

Capitalization

Consider yourself lucky! Before the invention of the printing press (in 1430), no one thought about the size of letters. No one had a reason to think about how letter size would impede reading. However, when the printing press began to serve a much larger population and literacy improved, rules followed.

Rules for Capitalization

Although there are many capitalization rules, writers today use capitals much less than writers did at earlier times in the history of English. In fact, in the 18th century, every noun was capitalized:

My Children go to School by Bus each Morning.

The English language is always striving to simplify; dropping excessive capitals was a sensible way to start. Now we are committed to capitalization as a way to clarify communication.

With that in mind, learn the following rules. You'll find that most are simply logical.

1. Capitalize the first letter of the first word in a sentence.

   That seems easy.

2. Capitalize the first word in a new line of poetry if the poet has capitalized it.

   Once upon a midnight dreary, while I pondered, weak and weary,

   Over many a quaint and curious volume of forgotten lore . . .

   This line is quoted from "The Raven," a poem by Edgar Allan Poe.

115

3. Capitalize the pronoun *I* and the exclamation *Oh* if it is the first word in a sentence.

   Dan and I joined that organization years ago.

   Ellie heard her mother cry out, "Oh, don't drive if you're sleepy!"

4. Capitalize place names, street names, the deity, people's names and initials, languages, organization names, and specific course names.

   Italian I, Massachusetts, Oceanwoods Drive, Allah, Stephen J. Lerner, Red Cross, Palace Theater, Pacific Ocean

5. Capitalize days, months, holidays, and special days.

   Tuesday, June, Easter, New Year's Day, Presidents' Day

6. Capitalize *Mother, Dad*, and other words for family relationships when they are used in place of the person's name. The test for whether you need a capital letter is to see if you can replace the word with the person's name.

   All through school, Dad is the one who supported me.

   All through school, Lawrence is the one who supported me.

   If the sentence is wrong when you replace a word such as *Mom* or *Grandpa* with the person's name, do not capitalize.

   My father works for a construction company.

   You wouldn't say *My Lawrence* works for a construction company, so don't capitalize *father* in this case.

   Capitalize titles as well.

   Major Perkins led the parade.

 ## Practice 9.1

Indicate where capital letters are needed.

1. My birthday is in june; when is yours?

   _____

2. I'll meet you on Monday—martin luther king day.

   _____

3. texting seems to be making its own capitalization rules.

   _____

4. when we lived on parsons street, max lived next door.

_____

5. I've always said that mother never has to call me twice for meals.

_____

6. Main Street in east greenwich is being repaved.

_____

7. You're a great shopper, and i am looking forward to going shopping with you.

_____

8. two roads diverged in a yellow wood, _____

and sorry I could not travel both . . . _____

(Robert Frost, "The Road Not Taken")

9. We always have a big brunch on new year's day.

_____

10. i'm taking spanish I next semester.

_____

Back to the rules! Capitalize languages, areas of the country, and more.

7. Capitalize the names of languages, races, and nationalities.

Spanish, Asian, Bolivian

8. Capitalize geographic locations.

the Northeast, the West Coast, the Eastern Seaboard

Radio City Music Hall, the Southwest, Eiffel Tower

 Try not to make the common mistake of confusing sections of the country with directions.

We looked for a house in the Northeast for a year before we found one.

In this sentence, the Northeast is an entire section of the United States.

Turn north toward Broadway.

In this sentence, the word _north_ simply indicates a compass direction (north, east, south, or west). Therefore, a capital letter is not necessary.

9. Capitalize historical events, periods, and documents. Note that minor words such as *and*, *or*, and *the* are not capitalized.

Declaration of Independence, World War I, Magna Carta, Middle Ages

In the first term, Declaration Of Independence would be incorrect because *of* is a small word.

10. Capitalize names of businesses.

IBM, ACC Contractors, Inc., Ford Motor Company

11. Capitalize religions and their followers. Also capitalize religious terms for sacred people and things.

Christianity, Christian; Buddhism, Buddhist; Islam, Muslim

Christ, the Buddha, Allah, the Bible, the Koran

12. Capitalize Roman numerals and the letters of the major topics in an outline.

I, II, III, IV, A, B, C

   I. The Executive Branch

      A. The President

      B. The Cabinet

  II. The Legislative Branch

      A. The House

      B. The Senate

 III. The Judicial Branch

      A. The Supreme Court

      B. The lower courts

 ## Practice 9.2

Insert capital letters where they are needed.

1. He was lucky enough to get a summer internship with general electric.

2. We spent an entire semester studying the civil war.

3. I have yet to tour the statue of liberty.

4. I love the southwest for its scenery and food.

5. Have you ever studied the poets of the romantic era?

6. I usually collect donations for the American red cross.

7. After much soul searching, my friend became a buddhist.

8. My favorite area of the country is the southwest.

9. The book the battle for spain was very helpful for my research assignment on the spanish civil war.

10. The story of the declaration of independence is one of the most interesting in american history.

More Rules!

You've covered a great deal of ground in capitalization. Quotations, titles, and brand names bring this section to a close. Don't give up!

13. Capitalize the first word of a direct quotation.

    The fireman yelled, "Get out of the building now!"

14. In a broken quotation, capitalize the first word of the second part of the quotation only if it starts a new sentence.

    "Get out of the building now!" he yelled. "You have only minutes before the roof collapses."

15. Capitalize titles if they precede proper names, but not when they follow proper names or are used alone.

    Superintendent Kelly, Mr. Kelly, superintendent

16. Capitalize the titles of books, plays, and films. Do not capitalize the unimportant words such as *and* and *of* in these titles.

    Romeo and Juliet, To Kill a Mockingbird, Diary of a Wimpy Kid

17. Capitalize brand names but not general terms for products.

    Kleenex tissues, Chevrolet sedan, Dell laptop computer

Practice 9.3

Insert or delete capital letters as necessary.

1. Ms. Dorman, Superintendent of schools suggested a dress code for the high school.

2. I heard Anita whisper, "there's someone in here." Then there was silence, followed by a loud "who's there?"

3. *animal talk* is a book that takes animal communication seriously.

4. We took part in an activity sponsored by the organization called walk for a cure.

5. I start every day by reading *usa today*.

6. I hope to buy a new car, a ford, within the next six months.

7. "When you hear my car arrive," she said, "Please open the garage door."

8. Did you see the long-running play *wicked*?

9. I just reread the adventures of oliver twist

10. Ask superintendent Davis before you add any more space to this building.

Practice 9.4

Insert or delete capital letters according to the rules.

1. His trip to the west made him realize that he wanted to live there.

2. A fascinating part of our History course centered on the industrial revolution.

3. Great movies have been made about the declaration of independence.

4. "I'll meet you at 5 p.m.," she said, And he knew she wouldn't be on time.

5. I'm taking a swimming class on mondays, wednesdays, and fridays.

6. My parents said i could stay in bed for breakfast.

7. She cried, "oh, don't disappoint me again!"

8. My Father is a really busy man.

9. In addition to english, we're studying spanish and hebrew.

10. We're so impressed with the work that representative Alex Kelly is doing in our legislature.

10

Using Words Correctly

When it comes to errors in word usage, there is a possibility for error in more than one way. You might simply use the incorrect word. You might, for example, choose the word *aggravate* (make worse) when you really mean *annoy* (infuriate). Entire books have been written on this subject.

Common Errors

Some words are easily confused because they sound alike or look alike. These words are called homonyms, homophones, and homographs. Don't feel daunted by these terms. You'll find that you already know many of the similar words and their differences. In addition, the history of these terms—which come from the Greek—will help you to remember their definitions.

- *Homonym* comes from *homos* (same) + *nym* (name). Homonyms are words that are spelled alike but have different meanings. For example, *kind* can be an adjective meaning considerate and generous; *kind* also can be a noun meaning a class of things having similar characteristics.

  We learned good manners from our mother, who was a very kind person.

  Until we learned what kinds of foods—nuts, dairy—I am allergic to, eating was by trial and error.

- *Homophone* comes from *homos* (same) + *phone* (sound). Homophones are words that have the same sound for two different definitions. For example, *compliment* (meaning a flattering comment) sounds like *complement* (a verb meaning balance or go together).

  Why is it so hard to accept a compliment gracefully?

  Cheese is definitely a complement to macaroni.

121

- *Homograph* comes from *homos* (same) + *graph* (spelling). Homographs are words that have the same spelling but different meanings and sometimes different pronunciations. The noun *bow* meaning a hair ornament is pronounced differently than *bow* referring to the forward part of a ship.

  The puppy wore a red bow in its fur.

  I finally figured out that the bow was in the front of the ship.

Avoiding Errors

Distinguishing all the similarities and differences of homonyms, homophones, and homographs may seem difficult at first. Avoid errors by exploring their meanings and using them in sentences. You will find that you can do this!

Homonyms

The ultimate list of homonyms has probably not been written yet. The list is huge, yet there is no way to predict when another homonym will pop up. They simply exist as a large, useful, and important part of the English language. In addition, homonyms are great sources of jokes:

QUESTION: Why did the cat come down from the tree?
ANSWER: Because he saw the tree bark.

You will see homonyms presented in different ways. The first, and most obvious, is the list. Look at the following homonyms and their definitions to see if you are familiar with all of them. You'll find *bark* at the top of the list. Then put them to use in the exercise that follows.

bark: a dog's sound; the hard surface of a tree

bat: the only mammal that can fly; a club or heavy stick used in sports

fair: reasonable; an entertainment or exhibit

fine: not coarse; well

grave: needing serious thought; a hole dug in the ground for a coffin

left: departed; opposite of right

peak: pointed top of a mountain; tip of a hat

trip: stumble or fall; journey

wave: motion with hand; a ridge of water traveling into shore

Practice 10.1

Choose a homonym from the previous list to complete each sentence.

1. My goal was to reach Camelback Mountain's _____.

2. After we _____ the party, all the best food was brought out.

3. Every few minutes, I heard someone say, "Don't _____ over the tools!"

4. I said that I could be a great competitor in softball if only I had a good _____.

5. I told you. I feel _____!

6. Jack thought the car was priced right. The price was _____.

7. We had reason for _____ concern.

8. We had so much fun at the _____. We loved the scary rides.

9. We feel _____ concern for our soldiers.

10. A _____ flew into my attic; I had never seen a flying mammal before!

What do runners do when they forget something? They jog their memory. (Just checking to see if you were still with me, reader!)

Homophones

Three tomatoes are walking down the street—a poppa tomato, a momma tomato, and a little baby tomato. The baby tomato is lagging behind the poppa and momma tomatoes. The poppa tomato gets mad, goes over to the baby tomato, stamps on the ground, and says, "Catch up!"

Do I have your interest and attention? OK then, let's continue with homophones.

Homophones are interesting because they are pronounced the same way but are different in meaning and spelling. Read each row aloud, and you'll hear the same sounds, but you'll see the different spellings. Use a dictionary or the Internet to learn the meaning of any words with which you're unfamiliar.

Homophones

aisle	I'll	isle	
bases	basis	basses	
carat	caret	carrot	karat
does	dough's	doze	
palate	palette	pallet	
sew	so	sol	sow
their	there	they're	
yore	you're	your	

See Appendix B for a more exhaustive list of homophones.

Practice 10.2

Choose the correct homophone to finish each sentence.

1. All the musicians were in charge of (there/they're/their) own instruments.

2. If there's a missing word in the sentence, mark it with a (karat/carrot/caret/carat).

3. "Sorry, but (your/yore/you're) wrong!" she yelled.

4. I'm impatient for spring; I can't wait to (sow/sew/so) some seeds.

5. In this painting, Monet worked from a (palate/palette/pallet) of muted colors.

6. Can you tell us the (basis/bases/basses) for your decision?

7. If I (sew/so/sow) corn in that area, there won't be room for any other vegetables.

8. I want an (isle/aisle/I'll) seat.

9. May I use (you're/your/yore) pen?

10. I always put a (karat/carat/carrot) in my salad.

You may say these homophones sound absolutely the same—and you would be right. They do have, however, distinctly different meanings and uses. Still, the words *its, it's, there, they're, their, to,* and *too* are frequently misused. They're in the Common Errors Hall of Fame!

its	it's	
there	they're	their
to	too	

See if you can tell why the first sentence in the following pair is wrong:

INCORRECT: Its another rainy day.

CORRECT: It's another rainy day.

In Chapter 8, you learned that the apostrophe stands in for a letter. In the second sentence, *it's* means *it is*. That makes sense in this context. Remember that *its* is the possessive form of the pronoun *it*. There's no indication of possession in the first sentence.

The homophones *there* and *their* indicate place and possession. They sound the same, but the meaning is different, depending on how you spell them.

INCORRECT: My friends arrived at the airport and realized that they had forgotten there passports.

CORRECT: My friends arrived at the airport and realized that they had forgotten their passports.

In this example, you use *their* to indicate possession because you are describing the owners of the passports, not the location of the passports.

Often, the homophone *to* is a preposition that introduces direction; *too* is an adverb that means also or extremely. Correct the following uses of *to* and *too*.

INCORRECT: We're going too the plant store for supplies.

INCORRECT: We have to many supplies already.

Homographs

Homographs are words that are spelled alike but have different pronunciations and meanings. Changing pronunciation signals changed meaning, and that is why in lists of homographs they are frequently shown in a different form. Look at the word *affect*. It may be pronounced ehFEKT or AFFekt depending on the context. Capital letters indicate the stressed syllable. Notice the different pronunciation for each meaning of *minute*:

On this highway, exits are precisely one minute (MINNit) apart.

The difference between these two recipes is minute (myNOOT).

Obviously, changing pronunciation affects meaning. In the first sentence, *minute* refers to a unit of time equal to 60 seconds. In the second sentence, *minute* means so small as not to matter.

The following list of homographs gives the pronunciation associated with each word, expressed in the form used in the previous examples. Capital letters indicate the stressed syllable. Read through the list and look for differences in meaning. (From www.FictionFactor.com; reprinted with permission.)

affect: (ehFEKT) to change; (AFFekt) a person's feelings or emotion

alternate: (ALternit) the next choice; (ALternait) to switch back and forth

bass: (BASE) a string instrument; (BASS) a kind of fish

close: (CLOZE) to shut; (CLOS) near

desert: (dihZURT) to leave; (DEZert) arid region

dove: (DUV) a kind of bird; (DOEV) jumped off

excuse: (EKskyooz) to let someone off; (EKskyoos) a reason or explanation

house: (HAUS) a building that serves as living quarters; (HOWZ) to provide with living quarters

invalid: (inVALLid) not valid; (INvallid) an ill person

lead: (LEED) to guide; (LED) a metallic element

minute: (MINNit) 60 seconds; (myNOOT) tiny

perfect: (PERfekt) exactly correct; (perFEKT) to make correct

produce: (PROdoos) fresh fruits and vegetables; (proDOOS) to bring forth

record: (RECKord) a list; (reKORD) to write down

row: (ROH) a line; (ROUW) a fight

separate: (SEPerATE) to divide into groups; (SEPret) not joined together

tear: (TARE) to rip; (TEER) fluid in eye

tier: (TEER) layer; (TYer) a person who ties

wind: (WHINEd) to coil up; (WINd) the blowing air

wound: (WOOND) to injure; (WOWND) coiled up

Practice 10.3

Choose a homograph from the previous list to complete each sentence. Show the pronunciation as it is written in the list. The first sentence is done for you.

1. The puppies were <u>wound (WOWND)</u> around each other for warmth.

2. In my laundry, I always _____ the dark- and light-colored clothes.

3. _____ your score on this paper.

4. My friends know I'm afraid of heights. They would never _____ me when we're at the top of a mountain.

5. Please _____ the refrigerator door.

6. I'm trying to _____ my swimming stroke.

7. There is no _____ you can give me that will save our friendship.

8. The top _____ of chocolate cake is always the best.

9. Do you remember the song "_____ Your Boat"?

10. Many years ago, my parents bought some land in the _____.

Commonly Confused Words

Before we finish considering word problems, there is one more category of words that challenge readers and writers. This category includes words that sound *almost* alike but are, in fact, different in spelling and meaning. Sometimes we can blame these errors on spelling, but frequently we say or hear the words incorrectly. One pair of words that causes this kind of confusion is *advice* and *advise*.

Advice (a noun) is a recommended action, an opinion, or guidance you receive.

Advise (a verb) is to recommend or give counsel or an opinion.

In other words, *advice* is something you receive. *Advise* is an action someone takes. The following examples use each of these words correctly:

I only give advice when I'm asked for it.

I can advise you about that issue if you want me to.

Words That Sound Almost Alike but Have Different Meanings

WORD	DEFINITION	EXAMPLE
Accept	Acknowledge; agree to	I accept your gift with many thanks.
Except	Excluding	Everyone except Freddy arrived on time.
Adapt	Adjust to something	I can adapt to almost any climate.
Adopt	Legally raise another's child	We need more families to adopt hard-to-place children.
Affect	Influence something or somebody	An antibiotic will not affect a virus.
Effect	A result	Taking too many antibiotics may have an adverse effect.
All ready	Completely ready	Call me when you are all ready to leave.
Already	Before now	My friend Tim has already left.
All right	Satisfactory or all correct	It is all right to take the alternate route. (*Alright* is not an acceptable word.)
All together	Everyone in the same place	We'll be all together for the holidays this year.
Altogether	Totally; entirely	This course is altogether too difficult.
Allusion	Indirect reference	Only my friends understood my allusion to rap music.
Illusion	Mistaken idea	You have the illusion that I like vacationing in the country; I don't.
Climactic	Describing the point of greatest intensity (climax) in a series of events.	The dinosaurs' reign reached its climactic period just before severe climatic conditions brought on the ice age.
Climatic	Referring to meteorological conditions (climate).	

WORD	DEFINITION	EXAMPLE
Continually	Regularly or frequently	I am continually amazed at your academic ability.
Continuously	Uninterrupted	Any continuously loud noise in the street is annoying.
Emigrate	Exit a country	*Emigrate* begins with the letter *e*, as does *exit*.
Immigrate	Go into a country	*Immigrate* begins with the letter *i*, as does *into*.
Loose	Not firmly attached, slack	The loose tree branches were a danger to the neighborhood.
Lose	Misplace	If I lose another set of house keys, I'll scream!
Moral	Message of right and wrong	Children love stories that end in a moral.
Morale	Confidence; spirits	Shopping often lifts my morale.
Personal	Private; own	My bank account is my personal business.
Personnel	Human resources department; staff	My sister became a personnel director at that company.
Quiet	Silent; calm	I can only work when it's quiet.
Quite	Entirely	I'm not quite sure what you mean.

Practice 10.4

Use the preceding table to choose the correct word in each sentence.

1. I try not to discuss (personal/personnel) matters with friends.

2. After I finish my homework, chocolate candy is my best (moral/morale) booster.

3. The dog's barking never stopped; it was heard (continually/continuously) through the night.

4. I hope your cold will not (affect/effect) your ability to fly home.

5. Everyone apologized (accept/except) Erica.

6. The library was so (quite/quiet) I couldn't concentrate!

7. There were dozens of (lose/loose) tree limbs all over the street.

8. I found the novel was (all together/altogether) too long.

9. If you move, your dog can (adapt/adopt) to another environment.

10. I will always (accept/except) your (advise/advice).

Practice 10.5

Use everything you've learned in this chapter to choose the correct word to complete the sentences.

1. When was the last time someone (complimented/complemented) your cooking?

2. Our job is to keep the soldiers' (moral/morale) high.

3. I felt (to/too) weak (to/too) go to the gym after having the flu.

4. Jamal doesn't (quiet/quite) share your love of hard work.

5. If I can (adopt/adapt) a pet, I will.

6. The (whether/weather) hasn't cooperated this week.

7. We took a painter's (palette/palate) with us to the beach.

8. (Your/You're) too old for this game.

9. It's never correct to use the word (ain't/isn't).

10. Don't (pier/peer) out the window, please.

11

Spelling

At some time, we all wonder if our spelling is correct. For some people, however, spelling just doesn't come naturally; it's always a problem. If you are one of those people, you know you have to take special measures to improve. Read on for help.

Spelling Guidelines

You want to know where your strengths lie as a learner before you start a spelling improvement program. Knowing your learning style will speed the process and make it a more agreeable and lasting exercise. For example, are you a visual learner? Do you learn best by reading? Or are you an auditory learner, meaning you prefer listening? Or are you a kinesthetic learner—someone who learns best by doing? Determining the answers to these questions will help you become a better speller.

The English alphabet has 26 letters, but these letters make 45 sounds. This is a complication for some spellers because sounding out the letters doesn't always help. For example, the sound of *f* is not always spelled with the letter *f*. The word *enough* ends with the sound of *f*, but look at the way it's spelled! *gh* equals the sound of *f*.

In addition, the letters of the alphabet include both consonants (*b, c, d, etc.*) and vowels (*a, e, i, o, u*, and sometimes *y*). However, vowels have more than one sound, so sounding out a word with vowels is not always trouble-free. For example, the long *e* sound can be spelled in all of these ways:

be, see, meal, field

When in doubt, check your spelling online or in a dictionary.

As you will read later in this chapter, dividing words into syllables and taking note of accent marks will help you to become a better speller simply because you're tackling the problem one small bite at a time.

Spelling rules have to be a part of the conversation. Whether or not you find them helpful is a very personal opinion. Adopt the ones that are meaningful to you. Who doesn't love "*i* before *e* except after *c* or when sounding like *a* as in *neighbor* and *weigh*"?

Steps to Strengthen Your Spelling

To become a better speller, start by figuring out what kind of learner you are. Choose ways of practicing that match your learning style. Next, learn about syllables so you can break words into chunks that are easier to learn. Finally, learn spelling rules that will give you an edge in learning to spell many English words.

What Type of Learner Are You?

You want to take advantage of your strengths as a learner. Read the following descriptions, and think about which one comes closest to the way you tend to be most successful at learning new information.

If you are a visual learner, you remember information that you associate with words, pictures, or other images. You not only read your text, you take notes from it. You probably like any sort of visual help a text or teacher can give you—graphics or flip charts, for example. You probably love to read, and you should keep on reading! Devoted readers are frequently excellent spellers. When you study spelling, you want to see the word, spell the word, and see it again. To practice, make flash cards and use a highlighter, visual symbols, or designs to accompany the words. Obviously, if you are a visual learner who has experienced only oral presentation of spelling skills, or if your only way of practicing spelling has been oral, you will have struggled. Add visual techniques, and you will succeed.

If you are an auditory learner, you need sound to learn. You might associate what you're studying with music, whether it's a song or a particular beat. An auditory learner studies well with music playing. If your parents told you, an auditory learner, "Turn that music off and study your spelling list," they probably didn't know you were studying—and getting it done to music. In class, you learn from lectures and group discussions. Listening and speaking help you. You might want to record yourself dictating the spelling and then listen and repeat what you hear over a period of time. You may want to join

a study group or find someone with whom you can talk, study, and review lectures and notes.

If you are a kinesthetic or tactile learner, you are at your best when you are physically engaged in the activity. For example, you learn well in a lab setting where you handle materials to get information. Physical activity is the key for kinesthetic learners. Kinesthetic learners need to use special techniques to stay focused as they learn, and that includes learning to spell. Many kinesthetic learners prefer not to sit. They learn much more efficiently by walking back and forth with textbook, notes, or flash cards in hand and reading out loud.

To improve their spelling skills, kinesthetic learners can make flash cards for troublesome words. It may even help to add symbols or pictures—anything that helps you remember how to spell the word. Use highlighter pens in contrasting colors to emphasize trouble points in the word. Also, use your computer to reinforce learning through your sense of touch. Use your keyboard to create word lists. Dictate these to your listening device, and then listen as you walk or exercise.

Stressed Syllables

English has a 26-letter alphabet composed of vowels (*a, e, i, o,* and *u* and sometimes *y*) and consonants. In English, we combine consonants and vowels into *syllables*, or small units of sound. If the word has more than one syllable, there is an accent on one of the syllables. For example, study the word *alphabet*:

′

al-pha-bet

This word has three syllables, separated here with hyphens. The accent mark that appears above the first syllable tells you that the first syllable is stressed. Say the word aloud, and listen for the stressed syllable.

Which syllable is stressed in the following words?

con-so-nant

cor-rect

mean-ing-ful

If you chose the syllables *con, rect,* and *mean,* you were right.

You may wonder why you have to know about syllables. There are two good reasons. First, the ability to divide words into syllables makes it easier to learn spelling. Logically, words are just easier to spell in smaller segments, or

syllables. Second, learning about syllables will help you learn the meaning of some words. Some words have the same spelling but different meanings when a different syllable is accented. Think back to the homographs you learned about in Chapter 10. Do you remember MINNit and myNOOT? ehFEKT and AFFekt? To know the correct meaning, you have to know where the accent falls.

min-ute: a measure of time

I have only a minute or two to talk.

mi-nute: extremely small

How does she exist on such a minute amount of food?

Why Is English Spelling So Difficult?

Most English speakers and writers will admit that English spelling is sometimes odd and irregular. You understand why this is the case when you consider that English is drawn from so many different languages and that we've inherited spellings from the various languages. Add to that the fact that we had no dictionary until about three hundred years ago, so set spellings were not established until then.

Finally, English spelling is not always logical. For example, the sound of *gh* brings with it a classic story. Look at *gh* in the following words. Say the words out loud. How many different sounds do you hear?

bough

cough

sought

thorough

though

tough

through

The writer George Bernard Shaw—along with other spelling reformers—thought English spelling was so strange, he made up a riddle about pronouncing letters.

Using the sounds of *gh*, what does *ghoti* spell?

It spells *fish*.

How did Shaw account for that spelling? He argued that *gh* could be pronounced as it is in *enough*; *o* could be pronounced as it is in *women*, and *ti* could be pronounced as it is in *nation*. Shaw's riddle is just for fun because *gh* is pronounced like an *f* only at the end of a word, as in *tough* or *cough*, or after vowels, as in *draught (draft)*. When *gh* comes at the beginning of a word, it is pronounced the same way as the *g* in *get*; think of *ghost* and *ghetto*, for example. The other letters in *ghoti* also aren't pronounced in the most common ways: *o* sounds like an *i* only in *women*, and *ti* sounds like *sh* only when it is part of *-tion*, as in *nation*. It's complicated but true!

Spelling Rules

People have said that the only certain spelling rule is that there's probably an exception to the rule you're quoting. But don't get depressed! Find the rules that apply to many words, for example the rule about *i* before *e* (*relief*) or the rule about dropping the final *e* before a suffix beginning with a vowel (*hoping*). Read the following spelling rules, and decide which ones will be useful to you.

Rule 1: Adding a Prefix
When you add a prefix to a word, you do not change the spelling of the base or root word.

PREFIX		ROOT WORD		NEW WORD	MEANING OF PREFIX
il-	+	legal	→	illegal	not/against
ir-	+	responsible	→	irresponsible	not
pre-	+	pay	→	prepay	before

Note: The hyphen after each prefix indicates that a root word follows.

Prefixes have meanings. When a prefix is placed at the beginning of a word, it changes the meaning of that word. Study the meanings of these prefixes before you do Practice 11.1:

dis-	not/opposite of	ir-	not
il-	not	mis-	wrong/incorrect
im-	opposite of/not	un-	not

Practice 11.1

Choose a negative prefix from this list to make a new word. Notice that repeated letters do occur.

        mis-   un-   ir-   im-   dis-   il-

1. _____ regular

2. _____ mobile

3. _____ natural

4. _____ similar

5. _____ step

6. _____ legible

7. _____ appealing

8. _____ credit

9. _____ tie

10. _____ figure

Rule 2: Adding a Suffix

To add a suffix to a root word, in most cases do not change the spelling of the root word.

WORD	SUFFIX		NEW WORD	MEANING OF SUFFIX
honor	+ -ary	→	honorary	connected with
logic	+ -al	→	logical	pertaining to
teach	+ -eer, -er, -or	→	teacher	person who performs action

Before you do Practice 11.2, study the meanings of these suffixes.

-ize	to make	-able	capable of being or doing something
-ness	measure of	-less	free from
-al	pertaining to	-ly	occurring at a particular time; in a special manner; degree

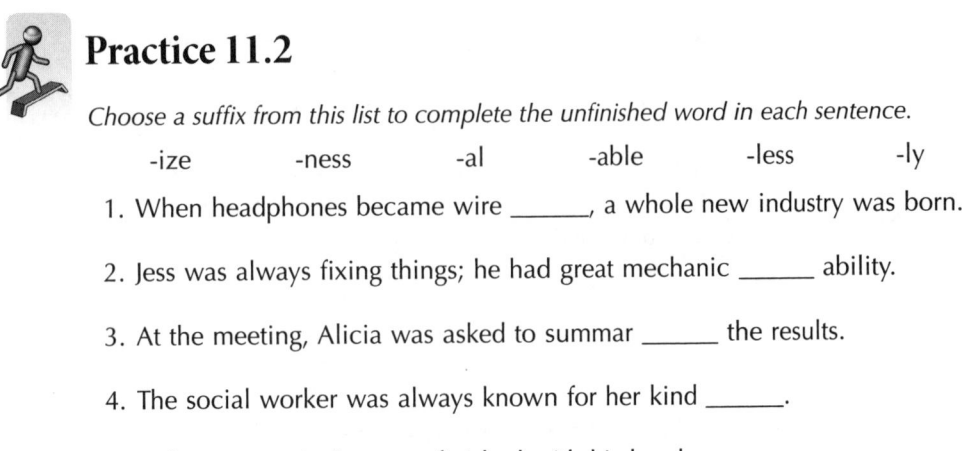

Practice 11.2

Choose a suffix from this list to complete the unfinished word in each sentence.

-ize   -ness   -al   -able   -less   -ly

1. When headphones became wire _____, a whole new industry was born.

2. Jess was always fixing things; he had great mechanic _____ ability.

3. At the meeting, Alicia was asked to summar _____ the results.

4. The social worker was always known for her kind _____.

5. Josh was practical _____ finished with his lunch.

6. That child is absolutely fear _____.

7. Her mother is known for her rude _____.

8. Fortunately, the large furniture we bought was mov _____.

9. This secret is strict _____ between us.

10. I will definite _____ finish my work by 5 p.m.

Rule 3: Adding a Suffix That Begins with a Vowel

When you add a suffix that begins with a vowel to a word that ends in *e*, drop the *e* before you add the suffix.

WORD	SUFFIX		NEW WORD
continue	+ -ous	→	continuous
fame	+ -ous	→	famous
guide	+ -ance	→	guidance

An exception arises with words that end in *ge* or *ce*. In those cases, you need to maintain the final *e* in order to keep the soft sound of *g* or *c*.

WORD	SUFFIX		NEW WORD
notice	+ -able	→	noticeable
courage	+ -ous	→	courageous

Here is an exception that avoids confusion with the word *dying*:

dye	+ -ing	→ dyeing

 There are notable exceptions to the rules in spelling. Here is one you should know. In the following two words, the *e* is dropped even though the suffix begins with a consonant.

true	+ -ly	→ truly
due	+ -ly	→ duly

Rule 4: Suffixes Change the Spelling of Words That End in Y

When you add a suffix to a word that ends in *y*, change the *y* to *i* before adding the suffix.

WORD	SUFFIX	NEW WORD
beauty	+ -ful	→ beautiful
happy	+ -ness	→ happiness

 ## Practice 11.3

In each sentence, use the preceding rules to choose the correct form for the word in parentheses.

1. His remark was (unnecessaryly/unnecessarily) curt.

2. Her (happyness/happiness) is my greatest concern.

3. The letter ended, Very (truely/truly) yours.

4. Merle needed (guideance/guidance) as she went through college websites.

5. Olivia was known for her (snappiness/snappiyness) when it came to her wardrobe.

Rule 5: Double the Final Consonant in a One-Syllable Word

The next rule is just for one-syllable action words that end in a consonant preceded by a vowel (for example, *plan*). To add a suffix to one of these words, double the final consonant before adding the suffix.

plan	planned
run	runner
stun	stunned

Practice 11.4

Choose a word from this list and add a suffix to finish these sentences.

occur   stun   plan   run   refer   sun   neutral

1. That accident _____ before I knew you.

2. I was _____ when I saw you!

3. We had _____ your birthday party for months.

4. I knew that Ramon and Samir were consistent _____.

5. I got the job after you _____ me to the manager.

6. When the ball hit my head, I was temporarily _____.

7. My raise was a totally unexpected _____.

8. Ceil was _____ herself on the roof.

9. A solar blackout is a rare _____.

10. Fresh lemon can _____ the sweetness.

Rule 6: Double the Final Consonant in a Two-Syllable Word

Sometimes a two-syllable word ends in a consonant preceded by a vowel and is accented on the second syllable (for example, *refer*). To add a suffix to one of these words, double the final consonant before adding the suffix (*referred*).

occur	occurred
occur	occurrence
refer	referred

Rule 7: Accent Changes

In a two- or three-syllable word, if the accent changes from the final syllable to a preceding one when a suffix is added (for example, when *refer* is changed to *reference*), do not double the final consonant.

prefer	preference
confer	conference
refer	reference

 ## Practice 11.5

Based upon Rules 6 and 7, correct the misspelled word in each sentence.

1. It never occured to any of us to check the weather report for our camping weekend. _____

2. What was your preferrence for dinner? _____

3. Our conferrence call took too long. _____

4. That was an occurence I'm not going to forget. _____

5. Your referrence to classical music started a great conversation. _____

Rule 8: *I* Before *E* Except After *C*

In English, many words include the letter combinations *ei* and *ie*. To help spellers decide which vowel comes first, someone a long time ago made up the rhyme "*I* before *E*, except after *C*." Notice how the following words follow this rule:

relief

receipt

niece

Unfortunately, the rule has many exceptions. Some exceptions are words that have the long sound of *a*, as in *neighbor* and *weigh*. Other exceptions include:

weird

seize

either

leisure

neither

Practice 11.6

Choose the correctly spelled word in each sentence.

1. Is your (neice/niece) your sister's child or your brother's?

2. I always have a great sense of (relief/releif) when exams are finished.

3. Always ask for a (receipt/reciept) when you pay your bill.

4. The theme of the movie was "(Seize/Sieze) the day."

5. Don't ever try to (decieve/deceive) Ray.

6. Tory stormed out saying, "You may not agree with me, but that is my (belief/beleif)."

7. We're so excited about what you've (acheived/achieved)!

8. Get out, (theif/thief))!

9. (Neither/Niether) of us is right this time.

10. If you call when you arrive, I will be (releived/relieved).

Rule 9: Forming Plurals

The basic rule for forming plurals is to add an *s* at the end of the word.

desk	desks
printer	printers

Other words form plurals differently, based on the word's ending. For words that end in *o* preceded by a consonant, form the plural by adding *es*.

tomato	tomatoes
hero	heroes

But if the words ending in *o* preceded by a consonant refer to music, add only *s*.

piano	pianos
alto	altos

For words ending in *y* preceded by a consonant, form the plural by changing the *y* to *i* and adding *es*.

sky	skies
story	stories

For words ending in *s*, *sh*, *ch*, and *x*, form plurals by adding *es*.

lunch	lunches
boss	bosses

For words ending in *-ful*, form their plurals by adding *s*.

spoonful	spoonfuls
mouthful	mouthfuls

To form the plural of a compound word, add *s* to the principal word.

mother-in-law	mothers-in-law
court-martial	courts-martial

The first term describes a type of *mother*, and the second term describes a type of *court*. *Mother* and *court* are the principal words.

With numbers and letters, form plurals by adding *'s*.

2	2's
c	c's

Some words keep the same spelling for singular and plural forms.

trout

deer

Chinese

sheep

Some words form their plurals by irregular changes.

alumnus	alumni
child	children
crisis	crises
knife	knives
leaf	leaves
datum	data
medium	media
thief	thieves
woman	women

Words Spelled with a *-ceed* or *-cede* Ending

Only three words are spelled with a *-ceed* ending:

exceed   proceed   succeed

Only one word is spelled with a *-sede* ending: *supersede*. All other words ending with a *seed* sound are spelled with a *-cede* ending.

Practice 11.7

Choose the correct singular or plural form for each sentence.

1. (Holidays/Holidaies) are always a welcome time in the school year.

2. I brought three (lunchs/lunches) back to the game for my friends.

3. We've had to buy two (pianoes/pianos) since I started taking lessons.

4. A truck (crashes/crash) into the guardrail every winter.

5. Your going with me (were/was) a great relief.

6. The children marched to their classes by (2s/2's).

7. Look at those blue (skies/skys).

8. We caught a basketful of (trouts/trout).

9. The scientist gathered a tremendous amount of (datum/data) for her report.

10. Too many (bosses/boss's) make working more difficult.

Practice 11.8

This exercise requires you to use everything you've learned in this chapter. Correct the spelling error in each sentence.

1. She said, "Carelesness is not an option." _____

2. Our knifes are all dull. _____

3. You'll succede if you practice a lot. _____

4. I've been planing the trip for a few months. _____

5. We had many more altoes than sopranos in the choir. _____

6. Two mother-in-laws took turns babysitting. _____

7. A family of six deers feed in our yard every morning. _____

8. My freinds are always very supportive of me. _____

9. Our town's war heros arrived home to a great welcoming party.

_____

10. Please turn in your 10s and 20s before you leave the bank. _____

11. Thank you so much for your job referrence! _____

12. I found that the steak was too tuff to cut with my knife. _____

13. No one has ever said that I am iresponsible. _____

14. Those four people were accused of being spys. _____

15. John was honored for being a couragous soldier. _____

16. That may not be ilegal, but it's definitely immoral. _____

17. I'm eating two more mouthsful of ice cream. _____

18. I'm so glad that you concured with my opinion. _____

19. I love the spelling of the word *wierd*. _____

20. That was a beautyful ending. _____

12

Writing Better Sentences

You've reviewed many aspects of correct English. Now you're ready to put your skills to work in writing the best possible sentences. There are a number of important but simple ways for you to improve your writing, and we'll explore them here.

Keys to Stronger Writing

Your writing will clearly improve if you avoid a few key errors with verbs, placement of words, and repetition.

- Remember that sentences are composed of subjects and verbs. When it comes to writing better sentences, your verb choice is especially important. In fact, you should choose action verbs as often as possible.

- Place important information at the end of the sentence. Placing important information last promotes sentence clarity. You can simply differentiate between what your reader already knows and the idea you're introducing. Explore that idea later in this chapter, in the section titled "Place Key Information Effectively."

- Place descriptive words and phrases correctly in the sentence. Adjectives and adverbs add color to your sentences, but they need to be placed correctly for clarity—ideally, close to the words they describe.

- Eliminate all unnecessary words and phrases in the sentence. Unnecessary words and phrases come in many forms. This frequent error must disappear first:

    My friend he is a much better athlete than I am.

Which small word stops the flow of the sentence and adds nothing to it? The answer, of course, is *he.*

- Balance your sentences with parallel constructions. In a balanced sentence, related ideas, descriptions, and actions take the same form.

   I decided that my eating habits and going to shop were two routines I would have to change.

How would you rewrite this sentence? Find the answer in the section titled "Balance Sentences."

- To show relationships among thoughts, use connecting words called conjunctions. Look back at Chapter 7 to review using punctuation and conjunctions to connect thoughts.

   We tried to mend our friendship a number of times; *however,* we could never find a basis for agreement.

- Every pronoun refers to a noun. Be sure the reference is clear.

   Millie told Gabriella she had a terrible cold and shouldn't go to the staff meeting.

Who has the cold, Millie or Gabriella? You will find clarification in this chapter's final section, "Seek Clarity."

Look at the difference a word makes when you use an action verb instead of a linking verb. Action verbs animate and enliven the sentence and eliminate unnecessary words.

LINKING VERB: The survey *was* done of all class members by the teacher.

ACTION VERB: The teacher *conducted* a survey of all the class members.

LINKING VERB: Their decision *was* to play their most experienced athletes at the end of the quarter.

ACTION VERB: They *played* their most experienced athletes at the end of the quarter.

Steps to Improve Your Writing

Attention to certain rules will immediately improve your writing. Learning to use active verbs, placing key information effectively, and deleting extra words are a few of the important steps you'll take.

Use Active Verbs

Simply stated, action verbs give your sentences more punch. Excessive use of linking verbs blocks sentence clarity. Do you recall the list of linking verbs

in Chapter 5? Avoid the overuse of this type of verb whenever you can. (That is not to say that you never use linking verbs. How else would I say, "I am happy, smart, and gorgeous"?)

LINKING VERB: A free book program *is* offered every spring by our library.

When you switch to an active verb, the sentence turns itself right-side up, so to speak. How do you do that? First, ask yourself who offers the program. It is the library, so *library* should be the subject of the sentence. Start with the subject and tell what it does:

> Our library offers a free book program every spring.

or:

> Every spring our library offers a free book program.

Assuming that the important information should come at the end of the sentence, the second sentence is the better of the two corrections. You want to emphasize the free book program, and that is what happens at the end of the sentence.

How would you improve this sentence?

> That was the first year that a win was achieved by our favorite team.

Start with the words *our favorite team*. Choose an action verb and finish the sentence:

> Our favorite team achieved a win for the first time that year.

or:

> That year our favorite team won for the first time.

Which version do you prefer? Did you notice that using action words results in slightly shorter, more concise sentences?

 ## Practice 12.1

Reword these sentences. Uncover the subject in each sentence and follow it with an action verb.

1. A black pen should be used to sign the documents.

_____

2. It is preferable to take a list of unread books to the library with you.

_____

3. It has been decided that I will take a part-time job.

_____

4. The price of gas was raised again this week by that gas station.

_____

5. It is a popular belief of many people that drinking milk will result in stronger bones.

_____

6. A new savings program will be introduced by the company this spring.

_____

7. As of January 2, Professor Kramer was in receipt of your letter.

_____

8. The order was processed too late by Carlos.

_____

9. One of the things that weren't working was the alarm clock.

_____

10. Building your endurance on the elliptical machine is the next step.

_____

Place Key Information Effectively

Placing the important or newer information at the end of the sentence promotes clarity. How is this done? Start with what your reader knows, and then add new information:

> After you have read the contract, place your signature only on the last page.

In this example, the reader knows about the contract. The new information is the need to sign the last page.

Place the key idea at the end of the sentence:

> If you are in an accident, file a police report.

The key idea here is that you must file a police report.

Practice 12.2

Reorder each sentence, placing the more important information at the end of each sentence.

1. Before the banks close today, let's open an account.

   _____

2. Go to the basement before the storm starts.

   _____

3. The huge interest in organic foods is an important topic.

   _____

4. Reread your research paper after being away from it for a while.

   _____

5. The need for alternative energy ideas in the United States exists.

   _____

6. In an organized way, this book builds upon what you already know.

   _____

7. The important issues were rarely addressed by the candidates.

   _____

8. Clarity is promoted by placing the important information last.

   _____

9. You should file a police report if you are in an automobile accident.

   _____

10. Because of your frequent late deliveries, we have switched to an overnight service.

    _____

Place Descriptive Words Correctly

As a writer, you must decide the meaning of your sentence and then place the descriptive word or phrase correctly. A very good rule is to place the descriptive word or phrase as close as possible to the word it describes.

! Misplaced Words and Phrases

To appreciate why every word has its correct place in sentences, read these confusing sentences.

I put some chocolate chip cookies in your lunch bag that I baked.

Did the writer really bake the lunch bag? Probably not. Just place the phrase *that I baked* where it belongs: after the word *cookies*.

Last year, I almost solved every math problem.

Last year I solved almost every math problem.

There is nothing wrong with either of these sentences, but which did the writer mean? Did the writer *come close* to solving every math problem, as the first sentence states? Or did the writer solve most of the math problems, as sentence 2 says?

Think carefully about the placement of descriptive words. Protect the meaning of your sentences!

Dangling Modifiers

A *dangling modifier* is a word or phrase that describes a word not clearly stated in the sentence. Exactly how does a descriptive word or phrase "dangle"? See if you can spot the athletic word maneuver in the following sentence.

Hiking the trail, the squirrels were all around us.

The dangling modifier is *Hiking the trail*. But who was hiking the trail—the hikers or the squirrels? According to the sentence, the squirrels were hiking. Not likely! The writer meant to say, "While my friends and I were hiking the trail, the squirrels were all around us."

A descriptive phrase becomes a *dangling* modifier when the word it modifies is not clear. In the sentence, *Hiking the trail, the squirrels were all around us*, it is not clear who is hiking the trail.

Let's repeat this important idea: Descriptive words and phrases have a correct place in your sentences. For clarity, place descriptions as close as possible to the words they describe.

What's wrong with this sentence?

The man in the park wearing a raincoat organized the crowd into two lines.

According to this sentence, the *park* is wearing a raincoat. Of course, that's not what the writer meant. Put the description with the thing described:

The man wearing a raincoat in the park organized the crowd into two lines.

The following sentence is even better:

In the park, the man wearing a raincoat organized the crowd into two lines.

The last sentence is more compact. It places the noun, the describing phrase, and what he did (organized) in the correct order.

Practice 12.3

Which words are misplaced in these sentences? Reword the sentences as necessary.

1. The dog belongs to the Addisons with the brown and white spots.

_____

2. The unlicensed truck drivers in the county office reapplied for licenses.

_____

3. The elderly man relaxed after working 50 years in his backyard.

_____

4. It was a happy day when I hung on my office wall my diploma.

_____

5. The car stayed in the driveway with the flat tires.

_____

6. We sat at the table, talking about our camping trip in the living room.

_____

7. In a ballerina's tutu, Simone photographed the tiny dancer.

_____

8. With the big, floppy ears, the dog walked briskly next to his owner.

_____

9. The child in his desk found his crayons.

_____

10. The ad said that a new set of chairs were for sale by a collector with modern legs.

_____

Delete Extra Words

When you edit your writing, look for all those extra words that clutter your sentences. Delete them. See if you can find the extra words in this example:

My reason for ordering in dinner instead of cooking is that we will have more time to talk.

Here's one way to simplify the sentence:

> Instead of cooking, I ordered in dinner so we will have more time to talk.

My (or *the*) *reason is that* is a much-overused phrase that does nothing but clutter sentences. Avoid it!

Also avoid meaningless and overused words and phrases: *quite, completely, utterly, utterly, at this time* (instead of just *now*), *up until that time* (instead of the simple *then*), *at that point in time, due to the fact that.*

EXTRA WORD: That sofa is quite comfortable.

Is the sofa comfortable or not? Say so! Delete *quite*.

SIMPLIFIED: That sofa is comfortable.

Here's another example:

EXTRA WORDS: We are not buying a new car at this time.

SIMPLIFIED: We are not buying a new car now.

 ## Practice 12.4

Simplify these sentences.

1. My English teacher he insists on and is quite a stickler for correct spelling.

   _____

2. Mr. Bergen utterly rejected my term paper.

   _____

3. When he asked me why the paper was late, I said the reason was that my dog ate the first draft.

   _____

4. Up until that time, I had succeeded with that excuse.

   _____

5. My mother she said my excuses were no longer acceptable to her either.

   _____

6. My reason for being late was because I woke up late.

   _____

7. When I was completely finished eating, I cleared the table.

   _____

8. Monica is quite intelligent.

_____

9. We became close friends at that time.

_____

10. Our car it is due for inspection this month.

_____

Balance Sentences

Why should you be concerned about balancing your sentences? The answer is simple: Balanced sentences allow your writing to flow smoothly. Indeed, they are much easier to understand. Consider the following:

UNBALANCED: The camp director said the program taught archery, kayaking, and how to swim.

BALANCED: The camp director said the program taught archery, kayaking, and swimming.

Do you recall the following statement in the beginning of this chapter? In a balanced sentence, related ideas, descriptions, and actions take the same form. In the unbalanced example, _archery_ and _kayaking_ are nouns. _To swim_ is a verb form. You needed to change the verb form to a noun—_swimming_.

Descriptive words also should be written in parallel form.

UNBALANCED: Our new car is faster, more powerful, and it's full of electronic advances.

BALANCED: Our new car is faster, more powerful, and more advanced electronically.

In the corrected sentence, matching _faster_ and _powerful_ with _advanced_ allowed us to delete the extra words _it's full of._

Practice 12.5

Reword the sentences to make all words and phrases parallel.

1. I heated the oven to 350 degrees, measured the dry ingredients, and then I was bringing out the eggs.

_____

2. This summer our family will paint our house, go to the beach, and we'll be reading as many books as possible.

_____

3. This new machine is neither faster nor does it cost less to use.

_____

4. Teenagers rank homework, lack of freedom, and being good at socializing as their major concerns.

_____

5. To find a summer job, search through job listing websites, ask your friends for ideas, and there are always employment agencies you can call.

_____

6. As leader of the group, you may be asked to write a report quickly and making it accurate.

_____

7. The basketball coach told the team members that they should sleep well, eat sensibly, and then they can do some warm-up exercises.

_____

8. Amelia likes baking cookies, icing cakes, and to make lasagna.

_____

9. Seth got in his car and he was driving away.

_____

10. He won the lottery, celebrated with his friends, and the next morning he would regret celebrating.

_____

 ## Use Connecting Words

Using connecting words adds meaning and clarity to sentences. You've already learned the simple conjunctions that coordinate ideas: *for, and, nor, but, or, yet, so* (many use the acronym FANBOYS to help them remember). This is how coordinating conjunctions work to show ideas that are equal in importance:

I will bring the sandwiches, and you can bring the drinks.

The traffic was very heavy, so Jake arrived tired and hungry.

If you instead need to say that one idea is more important than the other, you use a subordinating conjunction. When you use a subordinating conjunction, only one part of the sentence can stand alone as a complete thought.

> The ice on our roof melted because the sun came out.

Only *The ice on our roof melted* can stand alone as a complete sentence.

> When you come back, I'll have the shed painted.

Only *I'll have the shed painted* is a complete thought.

In Chapter 7, you learned to use punctuation correctly with subordinating conjunctions. However, there is another half to the story: Coordinating conjunctions add another level of meaning to your sentences. They add the concepts of time, reason, place, and more, as the following chart indicates.

Subordinating Conjunctions

TIME	PLACE	REASON	CONTRAST OF FACTS	CONDITION	MANNER
after	where	because	although	if	as if
before	wherever	since	though	unless	as though
since		so that	even though	until	how
when		in order that	while	in case	
whenever		why		provided that	
while				assuming that	
until				even if	
as					
once					

 Practice 12.6

Choose a subordinating conjunction from the chart to logically complete each sentence. More than one conjunction might work.

1. _____ you've been out of the office, I've finished all my work.

2. You can help me _____ you get back on time.

3. We can see that new movie _____ we have time.

4. You'll be promoted _____ your computer skills are so up-to-date.

5. _____ you get back we'll eat dinner.

6. _____ he ran around the track five times, David was too tired to play basketball.

7. His mother said, "You can't watch television _____ you finish your science project."

8. _____ Ruby is a good tennis player, you are even better.

9. _____ we don't get home in time, leave without us.

10. _____ _____ we arrive on time, we should get good seats.

Seek Clarity

Clarity in sentences demands that pronoun references be clear. When a pronoun comes later in a sentence but refers to something (called the *antecedent*) before it, that "something" must be clear.

UNCLEAR: The homeowner told the repairman that his air conditioner didn't work.

In this example, *his* could refer to either the homeowner or the repairman. Whose air conditioner doesn't work—the homeowner's or the repairman's? The sentence does not make that clear. Here is one way to improve the sentence:

CLEAR: The homeowner told the repairman that his, the homeowner's, air conditioner didn't work.

Try another example with a pronoun and two antecedents:

UNCLEAR: Our guests, Harry and Joe, arrived at 6 p.m., but he could only stay until 8 p.m.

Who could stay until 8 p.m.—Harry or Joe?

CLEAR: Our guests, Harry and Joe, arrived at 6 p.m., but Harry could only stay until 8 p.m.

Practice 12.7

Make pronoun references clear in these sentences.

1. Max and Evan moved the boxes to the third floor, but he said they couldn't stay there.

2. Each of the boys wants a car for themselves.

_____

3. On Saturday, my mother said, "Anybody in this family who thinks they are leaving before the house is cleaned are wrong!"

_____

4. Although the car hit the guardrail, it was not damaged.

_____

5. Dawn and Shaniqua were invited to the party but she didn't come.

_____

6. As soon as they arrived at the party, Katelyn and Marcella called her parents.

_____

7. The student used her pen to write a report in her notebook; then she put it away.

_____

8. A student can make an appointment with the teacher if they have any questions.

_____

9. Nancy told Maya that she had to get more sleep.

_____

10. After putting the antique bowl in the cabinet, Nancy sold it.

_____

Practice 12.8

Use all that you have learned in this chapter to eliminate errors and improve clarity in these sentences.

1. My reason for taking that course was that it was required.

_____

2. My boss she is difficult to please.

_____

3. At this time I'm too busy with school and work for socializing.

_____

4. Our plan is to make lunches for all, pack the car, and then we'll leave on time, too.

_____

5. Cari and Eden came with us to Arizona, but she had a sore throat the entire time.

_____

6. I left the suitcases untouched and my reason is that family members should take care of their own.

_____

7. Free swimming instruction is offered every spring by the community center.

_____

8. My father he is the best pizza maker of all!

_____

9. This computer is faster, more reliable, and you know it was cheaper.

_____

10. Ms. Ellison said my debate topic was quite interesting.

_____

Appendix A

100 Most Often ~~Mispelled~~ Misspelled Words in English

Here are the 100 words most commonly misspelled ("misspell" is one of them). Dr. Language has provided a one-stop cure for all your spelling ills. Each word has a mnemonic pill with it and, if you swallow it, it will help you to remember how to spell the word. Master the orthography of the words on this page and reduce the time you spend searching dictionaries by 50 percent. Reprinted here by permission. Copyright 2004, Lexiteria LLC and alphaDictionary.com.

A

acceptable: Several words made the list because of the suffix pronounced -êbl but sometimes spelled -ible, sometimes -able. Just remember to accept any table offered to you and you will spell this word OK.

accidentally: It is no accident that the test for adverbs on -ly is whether they come from an adjective on -al ("accidental" in this case). If so, the -al has to be in the spelling. No publical, then *publicly*.

accommodate: Remember, this word is large enough to accommodate both a double "c" AND a double "m."

acquire: Try to acquire the knowledge that this word and the next began with the prefix ad- but the [d] converts to [c] before [q].

acquit: See the previous discussion.

a lot: Two words! Hopefully, you won't have to allot a lot of time to this problem.

amateur: Amateurs need not be mature: this word ends on the French suffix -eur (the equivalent of English -er).

apparent: A parent need not be apparent but "apparent" must pay the rent, so remember this word always has the rent.

argument: Let's not argue about the loss of this verb's silent [e] before the suffix -ment.

atheist: Lord help you remember that this word comprises the prefix a- "not" + the "god" (also in the-ology) + -ist "one who believes."

B

believe: You must believe that [i] usually comes before [e] except after [c] or when it is pronounced like "a" as "neighbor" and "weigh" or "e" as in "their" and "heir." Also take a look at *foreign*. (The "i-before-e" rule has more exceptions than words it applies to.)

bellwether: Often misspelled "bellweather." A wether is a gelded ram, chosen to lead the herd (thus his bell) due to the greater likelihood that he will remain at all times ahead of the ewes.

C

calendar: This word has an [e] between two [a]s. The last vowel is [a].

category: This word is not in a category with "catastrophe" even if it sounds like it: the middle letter is [e].

cemetery: Don't let this one bury you: it ends on -ery, nary an -ary in it. You already know it starts on [c], of course.

changeable: The verb "change" keeps its [e] here to indicate that the [g] is soft, not hard. (That is also why "judgement" is the correct spelling of this word, no matter what anyone says.)

collectible: Another -ible word. You just have to remember.

column: Silent final [e] is commonplace in English but a silent final [n] is not uncommon, especially after [m].

committed: If you are committed to correct spelling, you will remember that this word doubles its final [t] from "commit" to "committed."

conscience: Don't let misspelling this word weigh on your conscience: [ch] spelled "sc" is unusual but legitimate.

conscientious: Work on your spelling conscientiously and remember this word with [ch] spelled two different ways: "sc" and "ti." English spelling!

conscious: Try to be conscious of the "sc" [ch] sound and all the vowels in this word's ending and i-o-u a note of congratulations.

consensus: The census does not require a consensus, since they are not related.

D

daiquiri: Don't make yourself another daiquiri until you learn how to spell this funny word—the name of a Cuban village.

definite (ly): This word definitely sounds as though it ends only on -it, but it carries a silent "e" everywhere it goes.

discipline: A little discipline, spelled with the [s] and the [c], will get you to the correct spelling of this one.

drunkenness: You would be surprised how many sober people omit one of the [n]s in this one.

dumbbell: Even smart people forget one of the [b]s in this one. (So be careful who you call one when you write.)

E

embarrass (ment): This one won't embarrass you if you remember it is large enough for a double [r] AND a double [s].

equipment: This word is misspelled "equiptment" 22,932 times on the web right now.

exhilarate: Remembering that [h] when you spell this word will lift your spirits, and if you remember both [a]s it will be exhilarating!

exceed: Remember that this one is -ceed, not -cede. (To exceed all expectations, master the spellings of this word, "precede," and "supersede.")

existence: No word like this one spelled with an [a] is in existence. This word is a *ménage à quatre* of one [i] with three [e]s.

experience: Don't experience the same problem many have with "existence" in this word: -ence!

F

fiery: The silent "e" on "fire" is also cowardly: it retreats inside the word rather than face the suffix -y.

foreign: Here is one of several words that violate the i-before-e rule. (See "believe.")

G

gauge: You must learn to gauge the positioning of the [a] and [u] in this word. Remember, they are in alphabetical order (though not the [e]).

grateful: You should be grateful to know that keeping "great" out of "grateful" is great.

guarantee: I guarantee you that this word is not spelled like "warranty" even though they are synonyms.

H

harass: This word is too small for two double letters but don't let it harass you, just keep the [r]s down to one.

height: English reaches the height (not heighth!) of absurdity when it spells "height" and "width" so differently.

hierarchy: The i-before-e rule works here, so what is the problem?

humorous: Humor us and spell this word "humorous": the [r] is so weak, it needs an [o] on both sides to hold it up.

I

ignorance: Don't show your ignorance by spelling this word -ence!

immediate: The immediate thing to remember is that this word has a prefix, in- "not," which becomes [m] before [m] (or [b] or [p]). "Not mediate" means direct, which is why "immediately" means "directly."

independent: Please be independent, but not in your spelling of this word. It ends on -ent.

indispensable: Knowing that this word ends on -able is indispensable to good writing.

inoculate: This one sounds like a shot in the eye. One [n] the eye is enough.

intelligence: Using two [l]s in this word and ending it on -ence rather than -ance are marks of . . . you guessed it.

its/it's: The apostrophe marks a contraction of "it is." Something that belongs to it is "its."

J

jewelry: Sure, sure, it is made by a jeweler but the last [e] in this case flees the scene like a jewel thief.

judgment: Traditionally, the word has been spelled judgment in all forms of the English language. However, the spelling judgement (with e added) largely replaced judgment in the United Kingdom in a non-legal context. In the context of the law, however, judgment is preferred. This spelling change contrasts with other similar spelling changes made in American English, which were rejected in the United Kingdom. In the United States at least, judgment is still preferred and judgement is considered incorrect by many American style guides.

K

kernel (colonel): There is more than a kernel of truth in the claim that all the vowels in this word are [e]s. So why is the military rank (colonel) pronounced identically? English spelling can be chaotic.

L

leisure: Yet another violator of the i-before-e rule. You can be sure of the spelling of the last syllable but not of the pronunciation.

liaison: Another French word throwing us an orthographical curve: a spare [i], just in case. That's an [s], too, that sounds like a [z].

library: It may be as enjoyable as a berry patch, but that isn't the way it is spelled. That first [r] should be pronounced, too.

license: Where does English get the license to use both its letters for the sound [s] in one word?

lightning: Learning how to omit the [e] in this word should lighten the load of English orthography a little bit.

M

maintenance: The main tenants of this word are "main" and "tenance" even though it comes from the verb "maintain." English orthography at its most spiteful.

maneuver: Man, the price you pay for borrowing from French is high. This one goes back to French main + oeuvre "hand-work," a spelling better retained in the British spelling, "manoeuvre."

medieval: The medieval orthography of English even lays traps for you: everything about the MIDdle Ages is MEDieval or, as the British would write, mediaeval.

memento: Why would something to remind of you of a moment be spelled "memento?" Well, it is.

millennium: Here is another big word, large enough to hold two double consonants, double [l] and double [n].

miniature: Since that [a] is seldom pronounced, it is seldom included in the spelling. This one is a "mini ature"; remember that.

minuscule: Since something minuscule is smaller than a miniature, shouldn't they be spelled similarly? Less than cool, or "minus cule."

mischievous: This mischievous word holds two traps: [i] before [e] and [o] before [u]. Four of the five vowels in English reside here.

misspell: What is more embarrassing than to misspell the name of the problem? Just remember that it is mis + spell and that will spare you the worry about spelling "misspell."

N

neighbor: The word "neighbor" invokes the silent "gh" as well as "ei" sounded as "a" rule. This is fraught with error potential. If you use British spelling, it will cost you another [u]: "neighbour."

noticeable: The [e] is noticeably retained in this word to indicate the [c] is "soft," pronounced like [s]. Without the [e], it would be pronounced "hard," like [k], as in "applicable."

O

occasionally: Writers occasionally tire of doubling so many consonants and omit one, usually one of the [l]s. Don't you ever do it.

occurrence: Remember not only the occurrence of double double consonants in this word, but that the suffix is -ence, not -ance. No reason, just the English language keeping us on our toes.

P

pastime: Since a pastime is something you do to pass the time, you would expect a double [s] here. Well, there is only one. The second [s] was slipped through the cracks in English orthography long ago.

perseverance: All it takes is perseverance and you, too, can be a (near-)perfect speller. The suffix is -ance for no reason at all.

personnel: Funny story: The assistant vice president of personnel notices that his superior, the VP himself, upon arriving at his desk in the morning opens a small, locked box, smiles, and locks it back again. Some years later when he advanced to that position (inheriting the key), he came to work early one morning to be assured of privacy. Expectantly, he opened the box. In it was a single piece of paper which said: "Two Ns, one L."

playwright: Those who play right are right-players, not playwrights. Well, since they write plays, they should be "play-writes," wright right? ~~Rong~~ Wrong. Remember that a play writer in Old English was called a "play worker" and "wright" is from an old form of "work" (wrought iron, etc.).

possession: Possession possesses more [s]s than a snake.

precede: What follows, succeeds, so what goes before should, what? No, no, no, you are using logic. Nothing confuses English spelling more than common sense. "Succeed" but "precede." Precede combines the Latin words "pre" and "cedere," which means to go before.

principal/principle: The spelling principle to remember here is that the school principal is a prince and a pal (despite appearances)—and the same applies to anything of foremost importance, such as a principal principle. A "principle" is a rule. (Thank you, Meghan Cope, for help on this one.)

privilege: According to the pronunciation (not "pronounciation"!) of this word, that middle vowel could be anything. Remember: two [i]s + two [e]s in that order.

pronunciation: Nouns often differ from the verbs they are derived from. This is one of those. In this case, the pronunciation is different, too, an important clue.

publicly: Let me publicly declare *the rule* (again): if the adverb comes from an adjective ending on -al, you include that ending in the adverb; if not, as here, you don't.

Q

questionnaire: The French doing it to us again. Double up on the [n]s in this word and don't forget the silent [e]. Maybe someday we will spell it the English way.

R

receive/receipt: I hope you have received *the message* by now: [i] before [e] except after . . .

recommend: I would recommend you think of this word as the equivalent of commending all over again: re + commend. That would be recommendable.

referred: Final consonants are often doubled before suffixes (remit: remitted, remitting). However, this rule applies only to accented syllables ending on [l] and [r], e.g., "rebelled," "referred" but "traveled," "buffered," and so on.

reference: Refer to the last mentioned word and also remember to add -ence to the end for the noun.

relevant: The relevant factor here is that the word is not "revelant," "revelent," or even "relevent." [l] before [v] and the suffix -ant.

restaurant: 'Ey, you! Remember, these two words (letters) when you spell "restaurant." They are in the middle of it.

rhyme: Actually, "rime" was the correct spelling until 1650. After that, egg-heads began spelling it like "rhythm." Why? No rhyme nor reason other than to make it look like "rhythm."

rhythm: This one was borrowed from Greek (and conveniently never returned), so it is spelled the way we spell words borrowed from Greek and conveniently never returned.

S

schedule: If perfecting your spelling is on your schedule, remember the [sk] is spelled as in "school." (If you use British or Canadian pronunciation, why do you pronounce this word [shedyul] but "school" [skul]? That has always puzzled me.)

separate: How do you separate the [e]s from the [a]s in this word? Simple: the [e]s surround the [a]s.

sergeant: The [a] needed in both syllables of this word has been pushed to the back of the line. Remember that, and the fact that [e] is used in both syllables, and you can write your sergeant without fear of misspelling his rank.

supersede: This word supersedes all others in perversity. This is the only English word based on this stem spelled -sede. Supersede combines the Latin words "super" and "sedere," which means to sit above.

T

their/they're/there: They're all pronounced the same but spelled differently. Possessive is "their," and the contraction of "they are" is "they're." Everywhere else, it is "there."

threshold: This one can push you over the threshold. It looks like a compound "thresh + hold" but it isn't. Two [h]s are enough.

twelfth: Even if you omit the [f] in your pronunciation of this word (which you shouldn't do), it is retained in the spelling.

tyranny: If you are still resisting the tyranny of English orthography at this point, you must face the problem of [y] inside this word, where it shouldn't be. The guy is a "tyrant," and his problem is "tyranny." (Don't forget to double up on the [n]s, too.)

U

until: I will never stop harping on this until this word is spelled with an extra [l] for the last time!

V

vacuum: If your head is not a vacuum, remember that the silent [e] on this one married the [u] and joined him inside the word where they are living happily ever since. Well, the evidence is suggestive but not conclusive. Anyway, spell this word with two [u]s and not like "volume."

WXYZ

weather: Whether you like the weather or not, you have to write the [a] after the [e] when you spell it.

weird: It is weird having to repeat *this rule* so many times: [i] before [e] except after . . . ? (It isn't [w]!)

Appendix B

Common Homophones

Let's start with a homophone pun before you attempt the next pages:

Seven days without laughter makes me weak.

Get it? Week? Weak?

This appendix offers a very long list of word pairs, but you can assume that you already know many, many of them. Look through the list and read the definitions. Target the homophones you're not sure of, and go back to them from time to time for review.

A

ad (advertisement), **add** (combine things)
allowed (permitted), **aloud** (audibly)
ant (insect), **aunt** (father's or mother's sister)
ascent (upward movement), **assent** (agreement)
ate (past tense of *eat*), **eight** (8, the number that follows 7)

B

ball (round thing, sphere), **bawl** (cry noisily)
band (group, musicians playing together), **banned** (barred, excluded)
be (exist), **bee** (honey-making insect)
beach (seashore), **beech** (deciduous tree)
bare (naked), **bear** (endure; mammal with large stocky body)
billed (gave a request for payment), **build** (construct)
blew (past tense of *blow*), **blue** (color; depressed)

board (plank), **bored** (uninterested)

bolder (more daring), **boulder** (large rock)

born (brought into life), **borne** (withstood)

boy (young man), **buoy** (marker in the water, keep afloat)

brake (a device that stops or slows a machine), **break** (fracture, shatter)

bread (food made from flour and water), **bred** (brought up)

buy (pay money for purchase), **by** (a preposition expressing a spatial relationship), **bye** (good-bye)

C

capital (assets; seat of government), **capitol** (building where the U.S. Congress meets)

carat (weight used for gems), **caret** (mark to show missing text), **carrot** (vegetable), **karat** (measure of gold content)

cell (basic unit of living things; range of a mobile phone transmitter; small room), **sell** (exchange for money)

census (poll; survey), **senses** (physical faculty, intelligence)

cent (common currency subunit), **scent** (fragrance), **sent** (past tense of *send*)

cereal (grain; breakfast food), **serial** (sequential; in series)

chews (grinds up food before swallowing), **choose** (select)

choral (performed by a choir), **coral** (hard marine deposit)

chute (shaft, tube), **shoot** (fire a weapon)

cite (quote), **sight** (view, vision), **site** (location)

coarse (rough), **course** (route)

council (board), **counsel** (advise)

currant (small dried grape), **current** (existing now)

D

dear (beloved, prized), **deer** (animal with antlers)

dew (water droplets), **do** (act, see to), **due** (owing)

die (stop living), **dye** (coloring)

disc (in computer science, another spelling of *disk*, or recording), **disk** (part between bones of the spine)

discreet (tactful), **discrete** (completely separate)

discussed (talked over), **disgust** (revulsion)

doe (deer), **dough** (mixture of flour and water; money)

E

ewe (female sheep), **you** (person being addressed)

F

feat (achievement), **feet** (part of the legs)

find (discover something), **fined** (punished by imposing a payment)

fir (evergreen), **fur** (animal hair)

flea (bug), **flee** (run away)

flew (past tense of *fly*), **flu** (influenza), **flue** (smoke or heat outlet)

for (preposition meaning "in favor of"), **fore** (front), **four** (the number 4)

foul (unclean, unpleasant), **fowl** (chicken)

G

grate (bars in front of fire; make into small pieces), **great** (large in number; important)

H

heal (make well), **heel** (back of foot), **he'll** (he will)

heard (past tense of *hear*), **herd** (a large group of animals)

higher (above something else), **hire** (give somebody work)

hoarse (harsh, grating, in reference to a voice), **horse** (four-legged animal)

hole (opening, cavity), **whole** (undivided, complete)

hour (60 minutes), **our** (belonging to us)

I

idle (not working or in use), **idol** (object of worship)

incite (provoke), **insight** (clear perception)

its (indicating possession), **it's** (contraction for *it is*)

J

jeans (denim pants), **genes** (basic unit of heredity)

K

knead (work dough until smooth), **need** (require something essential)

knew (past tense of *know*), **new** (recently made, recently discovered)

know (comprehend something), **no** (indicating the negative)

knows (familiar with), **nose** (organ of smell), **no's** (more than one objection)

knot (object made by tying), **not** (indicating "opposite")

L

led (guided; past tense of *lead*), **lead** (chemical element)

leased (rented), **least** (smallest amount possible)

lessen (reduce), **lesson** (instruction)

lie (deliberately say something untrue; recline), **lye** (strong chemical cleaner)

links (associations), **lynx** (short-tailed wildcat)

load (something carried or transported), **lode** (deposit of ore; abundant supply), **lowed** (mooed, the past tense of a cow making a "moo" sound)

loan (money lent), **lone** (only)

loot (stolen goods; steal), **lute** (musical instrument)

M

maize (corn), **maze** (confusing network of paths)

manner (the way something is done), **manor** (noble's house and land)

meat (edible animal flesh), **meet** (get together)

mince (cut up), **mints** (pieces of mint-flavored candy)

miner (mine worker), **minor** (small; type of musical scale)

missed (did not hit a target), **mist** (thin fog)

morning (early part of day), **mourning** (period of sadness)

O

oar (pole used to propel a boat), **or** (otherwise), **ore** (mineral from which metal is extracted)

overdo (exceed), **overdue** (late)

P

paced (set the speed), **paste** (adhesive mixture)

pail (bucket), **pale** (light)

pain (ache, feeling of discomfort), **pane** (piece of glass in a window)

pair (two of a kind), **pare** (remove outer layer), **pear** (type of fruit)

passed (moved beyond, approved), **past** (what went before)
patience (endurance), **patients** (people given medical treatment)
peace (freedom from war; calm), **piece** (a portion)
peal (ring, referring to the sound of bells), **peel** (remove outer layer)
pedal (foot-operated lever), **peddle** (sell)
peer (gaze, stare), **pier** (dock)
plain (simple), **plane** (airplane)
plum (type of fruit), **plumb** (weight attached to line)
praise (admire), **prays** (speaks to God), **preys** (hunts someone or something)
presence (attendance; being there), **presents** (gifts)
principal (school administrator; main), **principle** (belief)

Q

quarts (amounts equal to one-fourth of a gallon), **quartz** (crystalline mineral)

R

rain (precipitation), **reign** (period in office), **rein** (horse's bridle)
raise (lift), **rays** (narrow beams of light), **raze** (demolish)
rap (make a sharp tap; a music genre), **wrap** (cover something)
reed (tall water plant), **read** (interpret written material)
real (genuine), **reel** (spool)
rest (relax), **wrest** (gain control)
review (look at something critically), **revue** (variety show)
ring (chime, encircle), **wring** (squeeze)
role (position, task), **roll** (turn over and over)
root (underground base of a plant), **route** (course)
rote (repetition), **wrote** (past tense of *write*)
rye (cereal grain), **wry** (amusing and ironic)

S

sail (travel by water), **sale** (opportunity to buy goods at discount)
scene (sight, view), **seen** (past participle of *see*)
seam (place where pieces join), **seem** (look as if)
seas (salt waters of the earth), **sees** (perceives with the eyes), **seize** (take hold of something)

serge (strong cloth), **surge** (rush forward)

sew (stitch), **so** (as a result), **sow** (plant seeds or an idea)

side (edge of a figure), **sighed** (made an exhaling sound)

slay (kill), **sleigh** (horse-drawn carriage used in the snow)

soar (fly), **sore** (painful)

sole (only; bottom of foot), **soul** (spirit, essence)

some (a number of), **sum** (total, money)

spade (shovel), **spayed** (neutered an animal)

staid (sedate, serious), **stayed** (remained)

stair (step), **stare** (long, concentrated look)

stake (thin, pointed post in the ground; bet), **steak** (cut of beef)

stationary (not moving), **stationery** (writing paper)

steal (take something unlawfully), **steel** (alloy of iron and carbon)

straight (not curved), **strait** (channel joining large bodies of water)

suede (leather with soft surface), **swayed** (swung to and fro; influenced somebody)

summary (short version), **summery** (warm)

T

tail (rear part of an aircraft or animal's body), **tale** (story)

taught (educated), **taut** (tight)

tense (anxious, stressed), **tents** (collapsible shelters)

their (belonging to them), **there** (an adverb used to indicate place), **they're** (contraction for *they are*)

threw (past tense of *throw*), **through** (movement from one side of something to or past the other)

throne (monarch's chair), **thrown** (past participle of *throw*)

thyme (type of herb), **time** (duration; to measure intervals)

tide (rise and fall of the ocean or other large body of water), **tied** (joined)

to (preposition indicating direction), **too** (also), **two** (2, the number following 1)

toad (amphibian similar to a frog), **towed** (pulled something along)

told (past tense of *tell*), **tolled** (rang slowly)

tracked (followed), **tract** (area of land or water)

trussed (supported), **trust** (have faith in)

V

vane (rotating blade), **vein** (vessel carrying blood to the heart)
vial (small glass bottle), **vile** (evil, despicable)
vice (immoral habit), **vise** (tool for keeping things immobile)

W

wade (walk in water), **weighed** (measured by weight)
wail (howl, cry), **whale** (large ocean mammal)
waist (body area between ribs and hips), **waste** (squander)
wait (stay), **weight** (heaviness)
waive (surrender a claim), **wave** (ocean ripple; to motion with the hand)
war (armed fighting between groups), **wore** (past tense of *wear*)
ware (things for sale), **wear** (have something on one's body), **where** (adverb used to question place)
warn (caution), **worn** (showing effects of wear)
wax (polish), **whacks** (sharp blows)
way (method; route), **weigh** (consider; find the weight of something), **whey** (watery by-product of the cheese-making process)
we'll (contraction for *we will*), **wheel** (rotating round part)
weak (frail), **week** (seven-day period)
weather (climate), **whether** (word that introduces alternatives)
which (word that asks a question about a choice), **witch** (somebody with alleged magic powers)
whine (high-pitched sound), **wine** (alcohol from grapes)
who's (contraction for *who is*), **whose** (belonging to someone)

Y

yoke (animal harness; burden), **yolk** (yellow of egg)
yore (the distant past), **your** (belonging to the person spoken to), **you're** (contraction for *you are*)

Answer Key

Chapter 1   Always Right: The Complete Sentence

Practice 1.1

1. book	3. no object	5. sentence	7. branch	9. no object
2. window	4. truck	6. chickenpox	8. no object	10. postcard

Practice 1.2

The following answers indicate whether you need to add a subject, verb, or both. Then they show one example of how to complete the sentence by adding what was missing.

1. Add a verb. Example: The wasp flying around the deck *stung* Benny.

2. Add a subject and verb. Example: *We swam* away because sharks were seen close to the shore.

3. Add a subject and verb. Example: After packing the car and making lunch for the trip, *we started* our vacation.

4. Add a subject and verb. Example: Before you arrived and I called the school to find you, *we worried*.

5. Add a subject and verb. Example: *Herby eats* peanut butter and jelly on white bread every day.

6. Add a verb. Example: Kentucky *is* hosting the Derby.

7. Add a verb. Example: The tiny dog *was* standing guard and yelping.

8. Add a subject and verb. Example: When your mother called the doctor, *he answered*.

9. Add a subject and verb. Example: After we finished dinner, *we played* charades.

10. Add a verb. Example: In the dark, a menacing figure *was* walking behind me.

Practice 1.3

Linking Verb	Words Linked
1. is	Aunt Hattie, cook
2. are	Lisa, Miguel, and Dennis; friends
3. am	I, happy
4. was	Cape, vacation
5. were	dogs, winners

Practice 1.4

	Action Verb	Linking Verb	Subject
1.		was	I
2.	volunteered		you
3.	staggered		Jack
4.		is	Kelly
5.	has used		husband
6.	drove		she
7.	greets		dog
8.	likes		he
9.	begins		day
10.	have had		parts

Practice 1.5

Possible answers are given for completing the incomplete thoughts.

1. Flying in a very large passenger jet has been a goal of mine for a long time.

2. Landing on his feet, the cat walked away.

3. I was trying hard to pass the driver's test.

4. no error

5. Taking the trip to Walt Disney World required a great deal of planning.

6. no error

7. Graduating from the computer program was the first step in getting a job.

8. Steering the car around the deep pothole, I avoided a possible flat tire.

9. I stopped shopping and reversed the downward trend of my checking account.

10. no error

Practice 1.6

	Subject	Action Verb	Linking Verb
1.		prices	rose
2.	vegetables		are
3.	we	need	
4.	puppy	barked	
5.	we	will eat	
6.	you		were
7.	apples		are
8.	we	can take	
9.	dog		is
10.	She	races	

Practice 1.7

1. What is a run-on sentence? I need to stop writing them.

2. In our solar system we have eight planets, and I can name all of them.

3. I looked through Aidan's telescope, and I saw Saturn's rings.

4. It's noon; be sure to wear sun block.

5. I kept looking at her, but she never said hello.

Practice 1.8

1. Carlos is a skilled carpenter; he built his own home.

2. It rained for three days, so I almost canceled the camping trip.

3. Some athletes believe a jump rope is the best exercise; they think it is the best exercise for conditioning your body for sports.

4. First put flour in the bowl. Follow this with the sugar and finish with a pinch of salt.

5. Last summer I learned to surf, although I never thought I'd be able to.

Practice 1.9

1. I had so much to do today. First, I organized my desk, and then we had a department meeting.

2. Organizing the office and my desk took all morning.

3. Washington Irving is known as the father of the American short story. He wrote "Rip Van Winkle" and "The Legend of Sleepy Hollow."

4. As soon as he woke up, he knew something was wrong.

5. Because we've never met, I don't know what you look like.

6. The president had a busy day. First, he gave a major speech; then he led a discussion of the issues.

7. I'll expect you at 9 a.m. We'll have a meeting, and then Abby will join us at 3 p.m.

8. Whenever you get up in the morning, please make the coffee.

9. Call me. I'll be waiting in the office, and I won't leave until I hear from you.

10. He arrived wearing a heavy coat even though it was 80 degrees and the sun was so hot.

Practice 1.10

1. Jack and Harry (drive) much too fast.

2. I won't (drive or travel) with either of them.

3. Minnie and Maxie, our two kittens, (are) very mischievous.

4. You and I (will make) the posters and (hang) them up.

5. Mike and Jose, who are single parents and students, (study or socialize) every night.

Practice 1.11

1. noun, subject

2. verb, action

3. verb, linking

4. pronoun, subject

5. verb, linking

6. pronoun, subject

7. noun, subject

8. verb, action

9. nouns, subject

10. pronoun, subject

Chapter 2   More About Subjects, Action Verbs, and Linking Verbs

Practice 2.1

1. lists	3. post	5. pay	7. meet	9. are
2. drink	4. needs	6. shines	8. are	10. is

Practice 2.2

1. sit	3. skip	5. eat	7. fall	9. gather
2. take	4. sit	6. share	8. create	10. leads

Practice 2.3

The subjects are given in parentheses.

1. (dog and cat) are	6. (pie) tastes	11. (car) is
2. (chair and table) are	7. (he and classmates) appear	12. (boys) play
3. (Alex and Maria) run	8. (nothing) is	13. (uniforms) change
4. (Kim and friend) are	9. (one) is	14. (each) is
5. (one) is	10. (child) walks	15. (information) is

Practice 2.4

More than one answer may be correct. For example, in the first sentence, all of the possible helping words could work. The choice depends upon your meaning.

1. will be	3. should be	5. to be	7. will be	9. can be
2. can be	4. will be	6. should be	8. could be	10. will be

Practice 2.5

1. am	3. tastes	5. grew	7. were	9. taste
2. seem	4. were	6. looks	8. becomes	10. is

Practice 2.6

1. Bob and Julie (plural) play	6. flowers (plural) smell
2. Juan (singular) plays	7. band (singular) sounds
3. brother (singular) was	8. child (singular) looks
4. dancers (plural) stop	9. team (singular) races
5. characters (plural) appear	10. fence (singular) protects

Practice 2.7

1. Here's	3. She's	5. They're	7. wasn't	9. There's; That's
2. Isn't	4. There's	6. You're	8. Weren't	10. Wasn't

Practice 2.8

1. are	3. are	5. were	7. were	9. are
2. are	4. tastes	6. was	8. are	10. complain

Chapter 3   Descriptive Words

Practice 3.1

	Adjective	Word Described
1.	My new	neighbor
	old	dog
2.	The floppy-eared	dog
	slow, gentle	dog
3.	A heavy	snow
	our	plans
4.	The decaying	tooth
	painful	tooth
5.	tired, cranky	Aidan
	the	room
6.	Washington State	apples
	crisp	apples
	delicious	apples
7.	Three hungry	children
	a large	plate
8.	steadfast	Lincoln
9.	The generous	woman
	the	meeting
10.	brilliant	smile

Practice 3.2

1. easygoing, lovable
2. no comma needed
3. heavy, bulky
4. tall, dark, handsome
5. gory, tension-filled
6. no comma needed
7. creative, usable
8. hungry, tired
9. violent, loud
10. repeated, high-pitched tapping

Practice 3.3

1. My car is the newest of the three of yours.
2. Chris is the best gymnast in the class.
3. Her classroom is smaller than yours.
4. This room is the brightest of all.
5. That pond is the shallowest of any in this area.
6. That fish is the largest in the pond.
7. Aldo's story is the longest of any in the class.
8. no error
9. Did you foolishly want to be the silliest person in the class?
10. Our new dog is the tallest of any I've ever seen.

Practice 3.4

	Subject	Action Verb	Linking Verb	Adjective(s)	Noun(s) Described
1.	clothes		are	simple	clothes
				tailored	clothes
				preferred	clothes
2.	sale		is	storewide	sale
3.	Mario	streamed		a	movie
				romantic	movie
4.	He	loves		adventure	films
5.	snack		is	my	snack
				afternoon	snack
				big	snack

Subject	Action Verb	Linking Verb	Adjective(s)	Noun(s) Described
6. SpaceX™	designs		advanced	spacecraft
			huge	gain
			weight	gain
7. Aidan, Joseph		look	cheerful	Aidan, Joseph
8. They		are	the	students
			new	students
			eleventh	grade
9. video		was	your	movie
			favorite	movie
10. January, February		were	cold	January, February

Practice 3.5

1. The pleasant, older woman sat next to me.

2. The cool, clear water invited us in.

3. no change

4. no change

5. This year, voting was so much faster because of a knowledgeable, courteous team of workers.

Practice 3.6

1. ugliest
2. loudest, louder (depending upon the number compared)
3. more profitable
4. tallest
5. speediest
6. tallest
7. most boring
8. most appealing
9. most difficult
10. longest

Practice 3.7

1. comfortable
2. better
3. shrewdest
4. better
5. unique
6. common
7. easiest
8. worst
9. worst
10. efficient

Practice 3.8

1. I ate the *smallest* of the three pieces of cake on the plate.

2. A late and unprepared student interrupted the lecturer.

3. My backyard contains a huge un-mowed lawn. (No comma is needed.)

4. You should be more careful when you drive on icy roads.

5. I couldn't have found an *easier* game for us to play!

6. Your solution is unique. (Remove *more*.)

7. I thought last night's homework was the *worst* we've had all week.

8. Your answers were good, but mine were *better*.

9. The older you get, the *more difficult* it is to learn a foreign language.

10. A large, muscular dog protected us.

Chapter 4   More About Descriptive Words and Phrases

Practice 4.1

Several answers may be correct. Suggested answers follow.

1. neighborly   2. lonely   3. friendly   4. lovely   5. motherly

Practice 4.2

1. more likely   2. most likely   3. slower   4. fastest   5. quieter

Practice 4.3

1. Many of our camping trips have been *really* exciting.

2. I don't feel *well* today.

3. My friend draws *well*.

4. Melanie passed the swimming test *satisfactorily*.

Practice 4.4

Adverb	Word It Describes
1. mistakenly	chose
most	expensive
then	did(n't) buy

Adverb	Word It Describes
2. rarely	shop
together	shop
3. tightly	fit
too	tight
much	too
4. comfortably	continue
5. happily	slept
6. slowly	walked
carefully	walked
7. quickly	draws
8. undoubtedly	find
9. warmly	smiled
10. quickly	ran

Practice 4.5

Adverb	Word Described
1. really	beautiful
2. early	spring
3. very	dirty
4. so	fragrant
5. extremely	grateful
6. too	late
7. always	tired
8. aimlessly	drift
9. absolutely	sure
10. recently	painted

Practice 4.6

1. nicely   3. quickly   5. suddenly   7. good   9. quick
2. good   4. really   6. well   8. nicely   10. well

Practice 4.7

1. really	3. badly	5. badly	7. very	9. well
2. real	4. bad	6. really	8. really badly	10. good

Practice 4.8

1. of	3. on	5. between	7. above	9. under
2. at	4. around	6. near	8. into	10. with

Practice 4.9

1. The artist hung his most recent paintings on the wall.
2. The plumber slept on the porch hammock after hours of work.
3. The doctor found her glasses in her filing cabinet.
4. My old car in the driveway has traveled 150,000 miles.
5. The calico cat with the brown and gold patches belongs to me.
6. The cat with the white tail belongs to that child.
7. The senator made a negative comment about her colleague's family at a congressional meeting.
8. The little girl found the puzzle in her toy box.
9. Laura made chocolate chip cookies with extra nuts for her children.
10. May placed the lamp that she turned on next to the plants.

Practice 4.10

1. loudly	2. regularly	3. really	4. easily	5. frantically

Practice 4.11

1. loudly	3. well	5. really	7. badly	9. well
2. well	4. quickly	6. good	8. particularly	10. loudly

Chapter 5   Verbs Tell Time Perfectly
Practice 5.1

1. had promised	2. had	3. had	4. had	5. had commuted

Practice 5.2

1. Sydney has ridden her bike every day since she got it for her birthday last year.

2. Mica has worn that coat on cold days since she bought it five years ago.

3. Mr. Astrella has taught for 10 years and is teaching at the same school today.

4. Enrico has raised flowers for many years and raises them in his greenhouse today.

5. John and Erin have raised two children, and now they spend time traveling.

6. Eric stood last in line since he had arrived later.

7. Wendy and Liz babysat for us since we had moved here.

8. Mia has camped in our backyard since we moved here three summers ago.

9. You and she had commuted together for five years before she changed jobs.

10. Before the election, both candidates had promised prosperity for all.

Practice 5.3

1. Leon had washed the car before Priya arrived.

2. Women had voted for more than 75 years before the issue of women's rights took hold.

3. Ceil and Dick had moved before they sold their house.

4. Someone told me that you had studied English before you moved to the United States.

5. I had no cash because I had lost my wallet.

6. Susie had driven the rental car 100 miles before she realized she was late.

7. I had suffered the pain of a separated shoulder for a week before I called a doctor.

8. After we had bought the bedroom set, we saw the deep scratches on the headboard.

9. Paulie had resisted working out before he met Jeannie.

10. Ceil had babysat for us before she entered middle school.

Practice 5.4

1. As soon as I had said his name, I knew I was wrong.

2. Steve will have overspent his travel allowance before his boss checks the account.

3. Just before the class walked out of the room, Mr. Rumpler had noticed the book on the floor.

4. The car had sounded strange for several hours before it stopped running.

5. Leslie will have improved her English by the time she finishes this book.

6. Julie had added an extra cup of flour before she realized it.

7. I walked out into the rain and opened my umbrella.

8. By the time Amanda gets home, Essie will have cleaned the entire house.

9. As I walked through the doors, the ticket taker scanned my ticket.

10. The baby had cried for several hours before it developed a rash.

Practice 5.5

1. has   2. have   3. had   4. will have   5. has

Practice 5.6

1. You have run a five-mile race each year since 2020.

2. Ted, Mario, and Alicia have run a five-mile race each year since 2020.

3. All my friends have exercised for many years.

4. My cousin Vinnie has traveled across the country and has written a book about his adventures.

5. My neighbors Aisha and Darius and the dog have moved to California, and they are tired of moving.

6. Fortunately, you had perfected your organizational skills before you took that job.

7. I will have spent 60 nights in school before I get that diploma.

8. If I'm not cautious, our roof will have deteriorated badly before I have it repaired.

9. As we pulled into the outdoor theater, the heavy rain started.

10. Sammy will have been a traffic policeman for 25 years before he retires.

Chapter 6   Pronouns
Practice 6.1

1. her	3. him	5. he	7. him	9. him
2. Rohan and I	4. she	6. her	8. Scott and I	10. she

Practice 6.2

1. his, her, or their (depending on your knowledge of your neighbor's preferred pronoun)

2. its
3. It's

4. theirs
5. You're

6. its
7. Your

8. Its
9. their

10. mine

Practice 6.3

More than one answer may be correct.

1. your, his, her, or their (This is an example of how more than one pronoun might be correct.)

2. his
3. His
4. his

5. your
6. their
7. my

8. his
9. Your
10. her

Practice 6.4

1. decides
2. her

3. were
4. are

5. are
6. forget

7. was coughing
8. is telling

9. finishes
10. leaves

Practice 6.5

1. Who

2. whom

3. whom

4. Who

5. whom

Practice 6.6

1. his smoking

2. to Eden and him

3. Who is

4. Alex and I turned

5. its tail

6. their dinners

7. each has

8. my brother and me

9. to Elias and her

10. Allie and I started

Chapter 7   Punctuation

Preheat oven to 350 degress. In a food processor bowl, combine croutons, black pepper chili powder, and thyme. Pulse until the mixture is of a fine texture. Place this mixture into a large bowl. Combine the onion, carrot, garlic, and red pepper in the food processor bowl. Pulse until the mixture is finely chopped, but not pureed. Combine the vegetable mixture, ground sirloin, and ground chuck with the breadcrumb mixture. Season the meat mixture with the salt. Add the egg and combine thoroughly, but avoid squeezing the meat.

Practice 7.1

1. Yes, General White, please tell us how you feel about that.

2. Please walk the dog, take out the garbage, and lock the back door before we leave.

3. My son said, "I'll only do that after you tell me where we're going."

4. I was about to turn off the lights and leave, but you stopped me and asked a question.

5. If I could get a job, I would move to Mesa, Arizona.

6. no comma needed

7. I have finished my research paper, but I'm not sure if it is long enough.

8. Wednesday, I have to confess, is the worst day of the week for me.

9. I was leaving the gas station when the attendant yelled, "Lady, disconnect the hose!"

10. I especially like to plant colorful, fast-growing flowers.

Practice 7.2

1. No one will forget Brady's bravery in the war; he certainly earned the Purple Heart.

2. no semicolon needed

3. The contract you wrote is unfair to me; I can't sign it.

4. Tory missed another practice; she will be sitting on the bench at the next game.

5. My friend just moved here from California; she wants me to show her the sights.

6. no semicolon needed

7. Taste my sandwich; it is delicious.

8. no semicolon needed

9. I watched "Dancing with the Stars" last night; I was so happy that couple number 3 won!

10. I love a gentle rainstorm; raindrops on my window put me to sleep so quickly.

Practice 7.3

1. I made the dress myself; I proudly wore it to the prom.

2. Jamie's sure she wants to go; I'm waiting to hear from Matthew.

3. Are you ready for exams?

4. You infuriate me!

5. Cari will make the main course for dinner. I'll bring the dessert.

6. Choose from brownies, apple pie, cupcakes, and carrot cake for dessert.

7. I streamed three wonderful movies in one weekend.

8. Really, Charlie, how do you feel about going to summer school?

9. You sent the letter to Providence, Rhode Island, on February 15, 2022, didn't you?

10. Plumbers fix rusty, broken pipes.

Practice 7.4

In some sentences, more than one punctuation mark may be correct.

1. I don't like the new schedule; I'll wait for next term to sign up.

2. My cousin Geri, whom you met last year, arrived yesterday; and in spite of her 24-hour trip, she wants to see the sights today.

3. I waited too long to ice my ankle; therefore, it became swollen.

4. My youngest cousin, Jenna, went on her first plane ride to Orlando, Florida; and, of course, she loved it.

5. The plasterers planned to start work today; however, their plan was ruined when only two workers showed up.

6. Put the ingredients on your list, or you will surely forget them.

7. We'll take the 10 p.m. train. You take the earlier one.

8. Geometry, history, and English are taught in the morning, so I've decided to start going to bed much earlier.

9. I love music; however, I was never very persistent about practicing the piano.

10. Lowercase letters follow semicolons. Only proper nouns, such as names, are capitalized after a semicolon.

Practice 7.5

1. Marilyn, Joe, and Tim were my teammates last year.

2. Rick, do you remember them?

3. Some people talk too much. They're usually not too popular.

4. Stop, thief!

5. I expect to graduate on June 14, 2024.

6. Amory, president of her class, is very well thought of.

7. Walk, run, or sprint; but get here on time.

8. I've just learned that we're moving to Boston, Massachusetts.

9. Ryan, will you go with me?

10. The warm, moist cake was so delicious.

Chapter 8   Punctuation, Continued

Practice 8.1

1. My daughter said, "Please let me drive to school today! I promise I'll be home by 4 p.m."

2. "Please let me drive to school today," my daughter said. "I promise I'll be home by 4 p.m.," she continued.

3. The doctor warned, "Don't take antibiotics for every cold"; therefore, I stopped.

4. "How could you have been on time?" she asked. "You got up an hour late."

5. Charlotte asked, "Can you remember if Judy said, 'I'll be in at 1 p.m. today'?"

6. Once again the teacher reminded the class to upload our reports by Friday, place our names on the first page, and include a Works Cited page.

7. "Did you remember to return your books to the library," Ms. Blake asked, "or are you waiting to be reminded again?"

8. I read three mysteries, including *The Blade, The London Terror,* and *Mysteries of the Deep.*

9. When I said, "Meet me at noon," I didn't mean 1 p.m.

10. The job counselor said, "Bring a pen, paper, and recent job ads with you."

Practice 8.2

1. Dear Mom and Dad,

2. I can meet you at the mall at 11 a.m.

3. For our trip, bring the following: a sleeping bag, small cooking utensils, and a tent.

4. At the meeting, Sara placed a small pile of papers in front of each person: an agenda, a list of expectations for each member, and a list of dates for future meetings.

5. Prepare to complete these items each morning: turn on the computer, turn up the heat to 68 degrees, make written notes of messages from the answering machine.

6. I want a secretary who can do the following: answer the phone, take correct messages, and use Microsoft Word and Excel.

7. A first-aid kit should include these items: gauze, tape, and aspirin.

8. no change

9. There are three countries in North America: Canada, Mexico, and the US.

10. Remember three things: Take extra money with you, dress for cold weather, and call me if you need a ride.

Practice 8.3

1. This book's cover is badly torn.

2. The bear shook its huge body.

3. To dot your i's and cross your t's is a very old saying.

4. Don't wait for me; my plane doesn't arrive until midnight.

5. The children's department is on the third floor.

6. My dog's ears stand up straight when he's angry.

7. I read that, in many parts of the world, goat's milk is used more often than cow's milk.

8. The horse's saddle was old and much used.

9. It's Charlie's birthday.

10. We're amazed at how fast our dog gobbles down its food.

Practice 8.4

1. Our team won one championship during the years 2018–2021.

2. We plan on taking the Boston–New York train at 11:30.

3. no dash needed

4. We live on the Massachusetts–New Hampshire border.

5. I pay the bills—don't call me for money—and I'm broke most of the time.

Practice 8.5

1. I love chocolate-covered strawberries.

2. My father-in-law has always been overbearing.

3. I'll take twenty-two small mushrooms.

4. He's seen as an all-powerful influence.

5. We've used out-of-date equipment since I started to work here.

6. She has a low-budget job.

7. My computer expert fine-tuned my old computer.

8. We know that people should not have more x-rays than are absolutely necessary.

9. The ice cream was sprinkle covered.

10. Before the vote, did you know who the chairman-elect would be?

Practice 8.6

1. I've never shopped at the local malls (Westlake Mall, Macy's, Middleboro Mall Kohl's).

2. I love vegetables (green beans, broccoli, asparagus, yellow corn, and peppers).

3. We hoped to buy shoes made in other countries (Italy [Florence], France [Paris], England [London]).

4. Before you leave for school, remember to do this: (1.) Eat breakfast, (2.) Make your bed, (3.) Walk the dog.

5. Sharon finished all her chores in 15 minutes (or was it 10?).

6. Use a separate bowl for the dry ingredients (sugar, flour, salt).

7. Charles grew up in a big house (some two dozen rooms, six bathrooms).

8. I've lived in small towns (250 residents!) and large ones.

9. The captain said, "Plan on leaving the station within one minute (absolutely no longer than two) of receiving the call."

10. My first week's pay was three hundred dollars ($300).

Practice 8.7

1. These are the ingredients I need to buy: flour, sugar, and eggs.

2. I promised myself (no matter what else happened) that I would take a vacation.

3. The teacher said, "Don't forget the quiz on Friday."

4. The teacher said that there would be a quiz on Friday.

5. I haven't seen you in so long.

6. One of the table's legs is loose.

7. My dog licked its dish clean.

8. Take the New York–Miami train.

9. Harrison is the ex-president of our club.

10. The all-inclusive price is a bargain.

Chapter 9   Capitalization
Practice 9.1

1. My birthday is in June; when is yours?

2. I'll meet you on Monday—Martin Luther King Day.

3. Texting seems to be making its own capitalization rules.

4. When we lived on Parsons Street, Max lived next door.

5. I've always said that Mother never has to call me twice for meals.

6. Main Street in East Greenwich is being repaved.

7. You're a great shopper, and I am looking forward to going shopping with you.

8. Two roads diverged in a yellow wood,

   And sorry I could not travel both . . .

   (Robert Frost, "The Road Not Taken")

9. We always have a big brunch on New Year's Day.

10. I'm taking Spanish I next semester.

Practice 9.2

1. He was lucky enough to get a summer internship with General Electric.

2. We spent an entire semester studying the Civil War.

3. I have yet to tour the Statue of Liberty.

4. I love the Southwest for its scenery and food.

5. Have you ever studied the poets of the Romantic Era?

6. I usually collect donations for the American Red Cross.

7. After much soul searching, my friend became a Buddhist.

8. My favorite area of the country is the Southwest.

9. The book *The Battle for Spain* was very helpful for my research assignment on the Spanish Civil War.

10. The story of the Declaration of Independence is one of the most interesting in American history.

Practice 9.3

1. Ms. Dorman, superintendent of schools, suggested a dress code for the high school.

2. I heard Anita whisper, "There's someone in here." Then there was silence, followed by a loud "Who's there?"

3. *Animal Talk* is a book that takes animal communication seriously.

4. We took part in an activity sponsored by the organization called Walk for a Cure.

5. I start every day by reading *USA Today*.

6. I hope to buy a new car, a Ford, within the next six months.

7. "When you hear my car arrive," she said, "please open the garage door."

8. Did you see the long-running play *Wicked*?

9. I just reread *The Adventures of Oliver Twist*.

10. Ask Superintendent Davis before you add any more space to this building.

Practice 9.4

1. His trip to the West made him realize that he wanted to live there.

2. A fascinating part of our history course centered on the Industrial Revolution.

3. Great movies have been made about the Declaration of Independence.

4. "I'll meet you at 5 p.m.," she said, and he knew she wouldn't be on time.

5. I'm taking a swimming class on Mondays, Wednesdays, and Fridays.

6. My parents said I could stay in bed for breakfast.

7. She cried, "Oh, don't disappoint me again!"

8. My father is a really busy man.

9. In addition to English, we're studying Spanish and Hebrew.

10. We're so impressed with the work that Representative Alex Kelly is doing in our legislature.

Chapter 10   Using Words Correctly

Practice 10.1

1. peak	3. trip	5. fine	7. grave	9. grave
2. left	4. bat	6. fair	8. fair	10. bat

Practice 10.2

1. their	3. you're	5. palette	7. sow	9. your
2. caret	4. sow	6. basis	8. aisle	10. carrot

Practice 10.3

1. wound (WOWND)	6. perfect (perFECT)
2. separate (SEParATE)	7. excuse (EXSKyoos)
3. Record (reKORD)	8. tier (TEER)
4. desert (dihZURT)	9. Row (ROH)
5. close (CLOZE)	10. desert (DEZert)

Practice 10.4

1. personal	3. continuously	5. except	7. loose	9. adapt
2. morale	4. affect	6. quiet	8. altogether	10. accept, advice

Practice 10.5

1. complimented	3. too, to	5. adopt	7. palette	9. ain't
2. morale	4. quite	6. weather	8. You're	10. peer

Chapter 11   Spelling

Practice 11.1

1. ir-	3. un-	5. mis-	7. un-	9. un-
2. im-	4. dis-	6. il-	8. dis-	10. dis-

Practice 11.2

1. -less	3. -ize	5. -ly	7. -ness	9. -ly
2. -al	4. -ness	6. -less	8. -able	10. -ly

Practice 11.3

1. unnecessarily   2. happiness   3. truly   4. guidance   5. snappiness

Practice 11.4

1. occurred	3. planned	5. referred	7. occurrence	9. occurrence
2. stunned	4. runners	6. stunned	8. sunning	10. neutralize

Practice 11.5

1. occurred   2. preference   3. conference   4. occurrence   5. reference

Practice 11.6

1. niece	3. receipt	5. deceive	7. achieved	9. Neither
2. relief	4. Seize	6. belief	8. thief	10. relieved

Practice 11.7

1. Holidays	3. pianos	5. supersedes	7. skies	9. data
2. lunches	4. crashes	6. 2's	8. trout	10. bosses

Practice 11.8

1. Carelessness	6. mothers-in-law	11. reference	16. illegal
2. knives	7. deer	12. tough	17. mouthfuls
3. succeed	8. friends	13. irresponsible	18. concurred
4. planning	9. heroes	14. spies	19. weird
5. altos	10. 10's and 20's	15. courageous	20. beautiful

Chapter 12   Writing Better Sentences

Practice 12.1

1. Use a black pen to sign the documents. (In an imperative sentence, described in Chapter 7, the subject *you* is understood. The action verb is *use*.)
2. You should take a list of unread books to the library with you.
3. We all decided that I would take a part-time job.
4. That gas station raised the price of gas again this week.
5. Many people believe that drinking milk will result in stronger bones.
6. The company will introduce a new savings program this spring.
7. Professor Kramer received your letter on January 2.
8. Carlos processed the order too late.
9. Only the alarm clock stopped working.
10. Next, build your endurance on the elliptical machine.

Practice 12.2

1. Let's open an account today before the banks close.
2. Before the storm starts, go to the basement.
3. An important topic is the huge interest in organic foods.
4. After being away from it for a while, reread your research paper.
5. The United States needs alternative energy ideas.
6. This book builds upon what you know in an organized way.
7. The candidates rarely addressed the important issues.
8. Placing the important information last promotes clarity.

9. If you are in an automobile accident, you should file a police report.

10. We have switched to an overnight service because of your frequent late deliveries.

Practice 12.3

1. The dog with the brown and white spots belongs to the Addisons.

2. The unlicensed truck drivers reapplied for licenses in the county office.

3. The elderly man relaxed in his backyard after working 50 years.

4. It was a happy day when I hung my diploma on my office wall.

5. The car with the flat tires stayed in the driveway.

6. We sat at the table in the living room, talking about our camping trip.

7. Simone photographed the tiny dancer in a ballerina's tutu.

8. The dog with the big, floppy ears walked briskly next to his owner.

9. The child found his crayons in his desk.

10. The ad said that a new set of chairs with modern legs were for sale by a collector.

Practice 12.4

1. My English teacher insists on correct spelling.

2. Mr. Bergen rejected my term paper.

3. When he asked me why the paper was late, I said my dog ate the first draft.

4. Until then, I had succeeded with that excuse.

5. My mother said my excuses were no longer acceptable to her either.

6. I was late because I woke up late.

7. When I was finished eating, I cleared the table.

8. Monica is intelligent.

9. We became close friends then.

10. Our car is due for inspection this month.

Practice 12.5

1. I heated the oven to 350 degrees, measured the dry ingredients, and brought out the eggs.

2. This summer our family will paint our house, go to the beach, and read as many books as possible.

3. This new machine is neither faster nor less expensive to use.

4. Teenagers rank homework, lack of freedom, and successful socializing as their major concerns.

5. To find a summer job, search through job listing websites, ask your friends for ideas, and call employment agencies.

6. As leader of the group, you may be asked to write a report quickly and accurately.

7. The basketball coach told the team members that they should sleep well, eat sensibly, and do some warm-up exercises.

8. Amelia likes baking cookies, icing cakes, and making lasagna.

9. Seth got in his car and drove away.

10. He won the lottery, celebrated with his friends, and regretted it the next morning.

Practice 12.6

These are suggested answers. More than one choice could fit.

1. Since	3. when	5. Whenever	7. until	9. If
2. if	4. because	6. After	8. Although	10. Assuming that

Practice 12.7

1. Max and Evan moved the boxes to the third floor, but Evan said they couldn't stay there.

2. Each of the boys wants a car for himself.

3. On Saturday, my mother said, "Any of you in this family who thinks you are leaving before the house is cleaned is wrong!"

4. Although it hit the guardrail, the car was not damaged.

5. Dawn and Shaniqua were invited to the party, but Dawn didn't come.

6. As soon as they arrived at the party, Katelyn and Marcella called their parents.

7. The student used her pen to write a report in her notebook; then she put the pen away.

8. Students can make an appointment with the teacher if they have any questions.

9. Nancy told Mia that she, Nancy, had to get more sleep.

10. After Nancy put the antique bowl in the cabinet, a customer saw the bowl and bought it.

Practice 12.8

1. I took the course because it was required.

2. My boss is difficult to please.

3. I'm too busy with school and work for socializing.

4. Our plan is to make lunches for all, pack the car, and then leave on time.

5. Cari and Eden came with us to Arizona, but Eden had a sore throat the entire time.

6. I left the suitcases untouched because family members should take care of their own.

7. The community center offers free swimming instruction every spring.

8. My father is the best pizza maker of all!

9. This computer is faster, more reliable, and cheaper.

10. Ms. Ellison said my debate topic was interesting.

Index